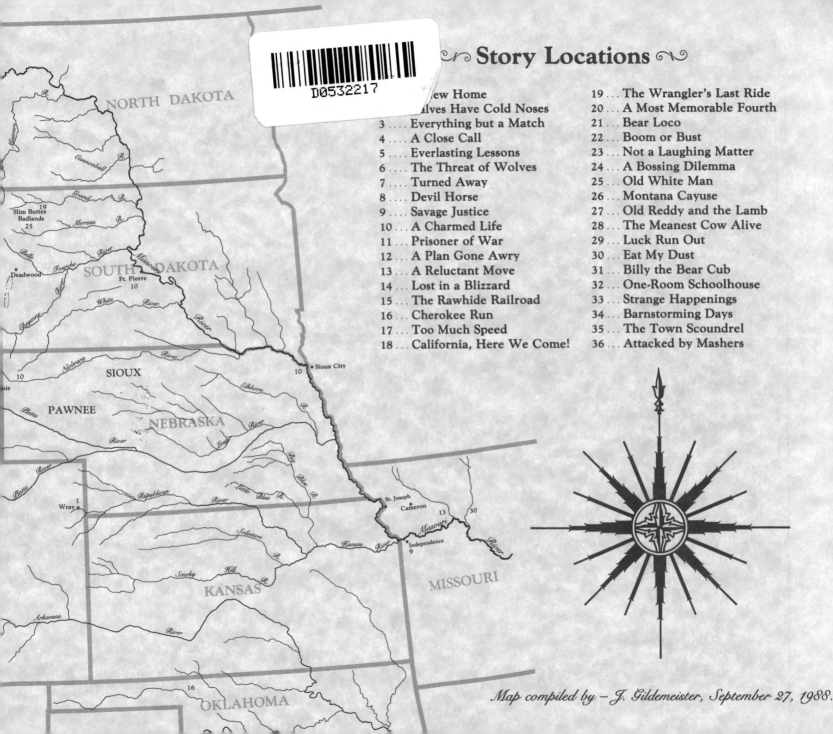

Story Locations

Map compiled by – J. Gildemeister, September 27, 1988.

A
Limited
First Printing

Jerry Gildemeister

An American Vignette

by **Jerry Gildemeister**

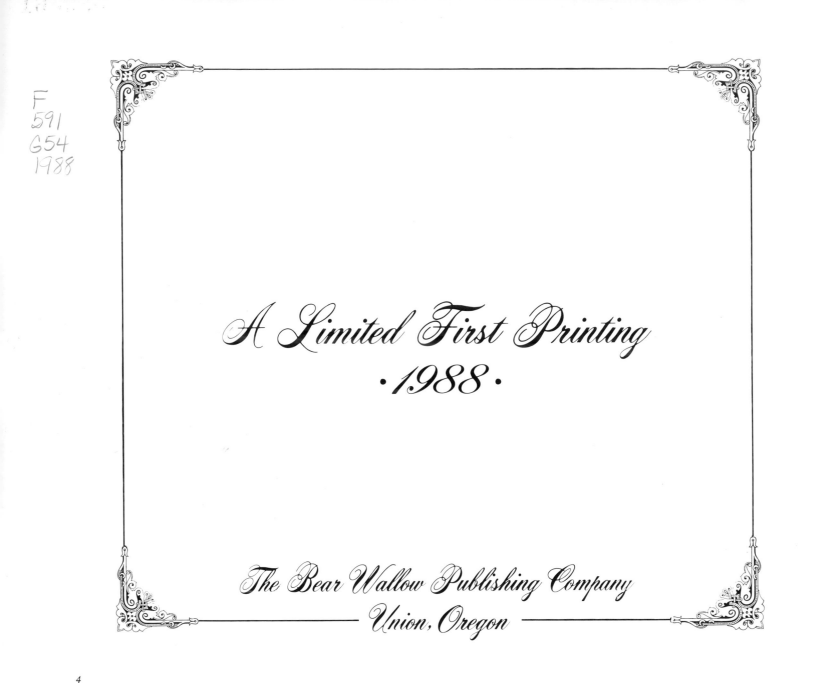

A Limited First Printing
· 1988 ·

The Bear Wallow Publishing Company
—— Union, Oregon ——

❧ About the Book ❧

Few people gave much thought to settling west of the Missouri River before the mid-1800's. When word reached the East of the free land to be had, gold to be dug, and untold opportunities to start a new life, the race was on. Out of all this activity came hundreds of thousands of adventures and experiences beyond imagining. Most have been lost with time, but some have survived down through the generations.

This is a book of stories and photographs that survived to reflect this epic history of the American West. They run the gauntlet from the peak of wagon train emmigration westward and the beginning of the Indian Wars in the 1850's, through settlement, skirmishes, traveling about, building the towns, and day-to-day living in the 1920's. You probably won't recognize the characters, but they are real. They haven't been immortalized in Hollywood pictures nor in print by the publishing magnates, for they are the *common folk* who didn't make the headlines or become notorious for their deeds. For the most part, they comprised a small segment of the population which struggled through daily hardships to carve a life out of the untamed wilderness we call the American West. These characters may never have gained great fame in the West, but they all have a story to tell. While some stories may have become embellished with age, that too, is part of the Western mystique.

We relished each new story and photo illustration submitted. It was sheer enjoyment to be able to blend words and illustration for a fresh look at an old subject. With our continuing goal of preserving our Western Heritage, we are proud to bring you.....

An American Vignette

Jerry & Cathy Gildemeister
The Publishers

❧ In Appreciation ❧

Through the generosity of all who responded to our quest we are able to share this special collection of stories and photographic illustrations in this 10th Anniversary commemorative to preserving our Western Heritage.

We owe a special debt of gratitude to the following for sharing these stories:

Margrita Balcom of Hilgard, Oregon— Maizie Carr of Belle Fourche, South Dakota
Eugene Clay of Yucca Valley, California—Lila Crawford of Corning, California
Dorothy Bruner Floerchinger of Conrad, Montana—Bessie Greene of La Grande, Oregon
Louise Choate & Vera Hearing of La Grande—Berenice Bue Juve of Moscow, Idaho
Carman Pearce of Redmond, Oregon—Edith Perkins of Mitchell Pass, Nebraska and Portland, Oregon
Jordis Schick of Salem, Oregon—June Schrib and Altamae Van Sant of Laramie, Wyoming
Marjorie Wilson of Beaverton, Oregon—Frederick Young of Cove, Oregon.

and the following for use of their picture collections to round out the book:

Neva McCord of Salem, Oregon for the O.H.P. McCord collection
Baker County Library of Baker, Oregon—Montana Historical Society of Helena
Nebraska State Historical Society of Omaha—Oklahoma Historical Society of Oklahoma City
Oregon State University of Corvallis—Union County Museum Society of Union, Oregon
Wyoming State Archives, Museums, & Historical Department of Cheyenne
and all others as listed in the Historical Notes of this book.

ᕚᕙ Credits ᕙᕚ

Writing, photography and design —
by Gildemeister.

Typesetting by Gildemeister.

Photographic print composing —
by Cathy Gildemeister.

Production coordination by —
Jerry and Cathy Gildemeister.

Text paper—Mead Signature Dull. End papers—
French Parchtone Cover. Supplied by —
Fraser Paper Company of Portland, Oregon.

Printing of book and end papers by —
The Irwin-Hodson Company of Portland, OR.

This book was bound by —
Lincoln and Allen Company of Portland, OR.

© 1988 **The Bear Wallow Publishing Company   Union, Oregon 97883**
—All Rights Reserved–
No part of the contents of this book may be reproduced without written permission of:
The Bear Wallow Publishing Company—Union, Oregon 97883
Printed and bound in the United States of America.

—Other Publications by The Bear Wallow—

RENDEZVOUS, *First Printing* © 1978 *(sold out)*.................ISBN **0-936376-00-7**.
RENDEZVOUS, *Second Printing* © 1978 *(sold out)*...............ISBN **0-936376-01-5**.
TRACES, *Limited Edition* © 1980 *(sold out)*.......................ISBN **0-936376-02-3**.
WHERE ROLLS THE OREGON, *Limited Edition* © 1985.....ISBN **0-936376-03-1**.
A LETTER HOME, *Limited Edition* © 1987...................ISBN **0-936376-04-x**.

Library of Congress Cataloging-in-Publication Data

Gildemeister, Jerry, 1934—

An American Vignette

by Jerry Gildemeister. —1st Edition.   p. cm.

Summary: A collection of true-to-life stories dealing with settling down, moving about, conflicts and skirmishes, and day-to-day living in the American West during the period of the 1850's through the 1920's, illustrated with historical and contemporary photography.

1. West (U.S.)—History— 1850-1925. 2. West (U.S.)—History—1850-1925—Pictorial works. 3. Frontier and pioneer life—West (U.S.) I. Title.

F591.G54 1988   978'.02 —dc19   88-10485 CIP
ISBN 0-936376-05-8:..... $29.50.

Contents

Settling In

The Dunham Wright Family of Medical Springs, Oregon.

The creak of wagons had hardly stopped before the air was ringing with the sound of axes as land was cleared and cabins raised. Smoke began to curl into the air; the pioneers were settling the Oregon Country and the Utah Territory. All needed shelter and sought protection. In the process, the Indian way of life would be changed forever.

The Raymond Hotel in the mining town of Bourne, Oregon.

Fortune seekers by the thousands followed the discovery of gold to northern California. Gold fever spread like wildfire to the Blues, the Rockies, and the Black Hills. Every new strike in the West transformed the mountains just a little bit more.

The U.S. Land Office in La Grande, Oregon.

Year after year, the demand for more land continued, each bringing new waves of settlers. Towns sprung up like flowers in spring. Land offices were doing a booming business.

Settlers and their sod house on the plains.

As treaties were broken, pioneers poured over the Great Plains frontier. Great cattle herds moved northward. Sod huts began to dot the landscape and barbed wire criss-crossed the open range. And the Indian was moved again.

A New Life

The slim young man, barely 35 years old, gazed out from the simple cab of the tractor he was steering along a country road in eastern Colorado. The year was 1918. He looked up and waved as the woman driver of a 1914 Model-T Ford swung her car around him without a stop.

He was Ernest Watt McIntire and she was Edna Jaquich McIntire, his wife. She waved too, as she passed him and continued on about three miles. She did not try to shout a greeting because the clanging piece of machinery drowned out all voice sounds in the still morning air. But the radiant smile each flashed to the other reflected the joy they felt and was adequate communication.

His piercing blue eyes, inherited from a father born in Ulster, Ireland, followed his wife's course until he saw her pull the car to the side of the road. Their plan was for her to kill the engine of the Model-T and wait for an hour or so until his vehicle came abreast of hers. Edna was one of the few women who drove a car in 1917. Mack had taught her when they first bought the vehicle because he thought a woman was as capable of driving as a man.

They were moving the tractor, a Rumley Oilpull rated at 15-30 horsepower, from Wray, a small county seat town on the North Fork of the Republican River, 25 miles south on the Beecher Island Road. The young man was pushing the tractor at its maximum speed of three miles an hour, while Edna was sometimes making around 20 miles an hour.

The couple had shipped their household goods via Burlington Railroad from Pawnee City, Nebraska, where Ernest had been a "tinner" and plumber. They planned to start a new life in Colorado. On tractor moving day their two daughters, June, who was two and a half, and Ruth, who was born in January, were staying in Wray with their Aunt.

When Edna stopped, she took up some embroidery work she had carefully wrapped in white tissue paper and laid on the back seat that morning. She enjoyed doing handwork of any kind and turned out exquisite embroidery, crocheting and tatting. More than that, she believed in using her time to good advantage.

When Mack, the nickname Ernest was known by, pulled up behind the Model-T, he throttled the tractor down, jumped to the ground and ran up beside his wife. "Dear, you don't know how great it is that you're helping me move the tractor," was his greeting. "And isn't it a wonderful ride? The air's so clear and cool."

He took a deep drink of water from the crockery jug wrapped in wet gunnysacking. "Do you want a drink too?" he asked.

"Yes, but didn't we bring a cup? How can I drink out of that narrow-necked jug?"

"Nope, you'll have to learn to drink from a jug if you're going to be a farmer's wife," he informed her. He jerked a quick splash of water over the mouth of the jug and held it while she drank.

"Mack, aren't we going through some kind of a little town soon?" she asked.

"No, remember, I told you it's just wide open space between Wray and the farm, no towns every few miles like in Nebraska or Illinois. But you don't feel smothered like I did in Minden or Pawnee." He took a deep gulp of the brisk air. "I just love it, and I hope you will too. "Scoot across here and let's look at the land stretching out for so many miles." As Ford cars of that era had no door on the driver's side, he opened the right hand door as she gathered up her ankle-length skirts and slid across the seat to get out.

Standing close beside her, he swept his arm across the width of the sky. "Look how far you see, Jakie," he said. This is a nickname he called her along with Wife or Little

Woman, all highly endearing because of the tone he used. However, to members of her family he always called her Edna.

Her response was, "But, Mack, what can you see when you look out there? For sure not trees."

"No, no trees right here," he replied, his exuberance undampened. "But we'll plant some trees at our place. I saw some little trees at a neighbor's house. Let's head on down the road, Little Woman. We'll take six miles in this hitch. Don't go more than 20 minutes or it'll take me too long to catch up."

He walked to the front of the Model-T and gave the crank a quick twist. She pulled the spark lever down and the gas lever up, and she was ready to step on the low gear pedal and start out again.

The prairie wind whistling through the car's metal framework threatened Edna's blond hair piled high atop her head, but she couldn't take her hands off the steering wheel to smooth it back. Mack had put the top up on the car that morning, but he hadn't attached the side curtains because he saw no threat of rain.

After awhile the road took a sudden dip down to a small stream flowing at the bottom of a low hill. A cautious driver, she stepped on the low gear pedal to cross the tiny rivulet and kept the car in low as it labored around a curve and up a long hill. At the top she stepped on the high gear pedal.

"The river Mack talks about has to be at the bottom of one of those hills ahead," she said aloud. A quick glance at the tiny gold watch she wore pinned to her shirtwaist told her she was at the crest of another slight descent with a clump of cottonwoods and willows at the bottom.

For a time she sat gazing at the endless prairie. The few trees near the stream ahead were the only ones she could see. The wind rippling across the brown prairie grass covering the low hills made a sighing sound. A vivid green growth showed on some level fields. Of course, that's wheat; that's what we're going to raise, she thought. We had wheat in Nebraska, but not such expansive fields.

Reluctant to step out of the car, she reached for the embroidery again. "I'll wait to get out until Mack comes in case I should see a snake," she said.

When Mack got there he made a beeline for the water jug, and she was glad to accept another sip. Once more he looked far off into space. "The crick at the bottom of this draw is Black Wolf," he explained. "Hit the narrow bridge over it square so you don't drive off the side. But keep on up the next hill, and from there it's an easy coast down to the Arikaree River. The place where we cross is called Beecher Island."

Suddenly he looked into the back of the car. "You did bring a lunch didn't you?" She nodded. "We'll eat at the river, rest a little while and go on to the farm pronto. It's only about ten miles from Beecher Island."

"Do you think we'll get there before sundown?" she asked.

"Oh, easy," he said. "I've got a bed made up, and I brought along some eats so we can have supper tonight. It's going to be great; wait and see."

"But will I have any neighbors? I've only seen a couple of farm houses since we left Wray." A child of a more settled region, she wanted friends in this new life.

"Yeh, we will. Shavers live only a couple of miles away. We can buy milk from them until we get a cow. Hop in. We're headin' for dinner this time."

"Mack, maybe I could crank the car, and I wouldn't have to wait for you to come," she suggested.

"No, Jakie, I don't want you to. You know the thing broke my arm when it kicked. That crank whirls back at you faster than you can let loose. We don't want a mother in our family with a *Ford arm*." He pulled the choke wire, gave the crank a quick twist, and the motor caught. They were on their way again.

As she coasted down the hill toward the river and steered over into the shade of a big cottonwood on the Arikaree's bank, Edna concluded Beecher Island would make a good picnic spot. She noticed a tall granite monument not too far away. Mack would know about it, she was sure.

She spread the blanket on the soft sand, set the picnic basket at the corner and waited for Mack to come. It was less than a hour until he came into sight and stopped a short distance from the car.

"This beast is so hard to start I'll leave it running," he said, "but the noise won't be so bad from this far away."

Strolling over to the blanket, he peered into the basket. "What've you got?" he asked. "I'm hungry as a bear."

"Thick bread and butter sandwiches, a full plate of fried chicken, a bowl of potato salad, and a cake Eda baked. That ought to be enough, shouldn't it?"

"Yes, I'll make out if we have an early supper," he replied with a grin.

He washed his hands in the river, wet the sacking around the jug, and sat down beside her. "The well's down, and the windmill's up on the place, so we'll have plenty of good water there. We can drive back to Wray in a little more than an hour tomorrow. I take these hills and curves a little faster than you do," he said in a teasing tone.

After they finished lunch, they walked over to look at the monument and discovered it marked the site of an Indian battle in 1869 where Lt. Fred Beecher had been killed. Mack remarked, "The Ekbergs who live around here told me the community has a reunion every fall in commemoration of the battle. Families bring picnics, there are church services Sunday morning, and a speaker in the afternoon. We'll come this fall," he promised.

"Now we're going on to the McIntire place. We'll take two goes at it. The long hill ahead is not too steep because the road winds a lot. When you get out on the flat at the top, you're on the South Divide, and Lansing Valley is right off to the east."

As Edna drove up what Mack called *the long hill*, she nearly lost her courage, although she took it in low gear. Being from Nebraska it was the longest climb she had ever seen. Indeed, it stretched nearly five miles from the bank of the Arikaree River to the edge of the divide where the McIntire farm was.

Occasionally she glanced back, but the only thing she saw was a cloud of dust kicked up by the huge tractor wheels. She gasped as she reached the top of the hill. "I'm never going to drive that hill again," she vowed, but in that prediction she was totally wrong.

The last stop was a short one with time only for a cool drink and Mack's advice. "Head for the cookshack and the windmill when you see them off to the southwest."

When she stopped the Model-T at the door of the cookshack, she realized why he had not told her more about it. The long gray building derived its name from its use with a threshing rig. The owner of a threshing machine and his wife lived in the movable shack during the long summer circuit from wheat farm to wheat farm. She cooked meals there for the harvest crew. It pre-dated the trailer house by decades and was anything but attractive.

Inside she saw a kitchen stove in one corner, a table with shelves above it, a bed on the opposite wall with more shelves beside, and a wire stretched across the corner to hold a curtain which created a makeshift clothes closet. The wash bench stood outside, but could be brought in during a storm.

After she carried the groceries up the wooden steps into the shack , she sank down on the bed and looked around.

"How will I keep enough food for four of us in this little space?" she wondered. "We'll go into Wray to stock up on groceries Saturday and we can see Ruth, if she has to stay with Eda. We can even take a bath. In between times we'll have to make do with a spit bath, I guess." She would bring a change of sheets, clean clothes, a pretty wall hanging or two to relieve the drabness, and June's crib.

When she heard the tractor clatter into the yard, she ran down the steps to greet her husband. As the huge engine slowly died, the prairie throbbed to the deep silence.

Together they looked out over the acres they had bought with money borrowed from a former employer. The sun hanging low above the western horizon streaked the limitless sky with shades of pink, orange, gold and mauve. Even the dun-colored prairie glowed with reflected light from the brilliant sky.

He was the first to speak. "Isn't it pretty?" he asked in a shaky voice. She knew he was close to tears. "It's a wonderful country, Jakie. You can see for miles and miles; you can breathe fresh air. I want to raise wheat on the plains of eastern Colorado. I can farm with power machinery; I don't have to plod along behind two old plugs on a little patch of ground in Illinois."

He pointed to the southwest. I'll break sod there first and drill wheat in the fall. You decide where you want the first half of the house because I'll start to build it next spring when the weather warms up. We can't stay in the cookshack for very long."

He looked down at her golden hair and soft face so dear to him. "Will you be happy, Jakie?" he asked.

She saw the dream in his eyes and knew she wanted to share it. "I'll be happy if you're here, Mack. You know that's what makes the difference for me."

He pulled off his cap, thumped the dust from it, and took her in his arms. "This is our new home, Wife. We'll live and die here."

Calves Have Cold Noses

It seems that keeping chickens on the farm has always had its problems: critters. If it wasn't weasels, skunks, or racoons, it was chicken thieves.

Around the turn-of-the-century, the neighbors to the Bruner family were losing chickens. Every few days some more would be missing, but they didn't know if it was from a four-legged or two-legged variety of skunk. So, one night when a noise came from the chicken house, the old man, dressed in his longhandle underwear and bedroom slippers, armed with a lantern and his favorite double barreled shotgun, snuck out to get the culprit.

While he was creeping up to the chicken house door, ready for anything that might run out, a pet calf slipped up from behind and stuck his cold, wet nose into the trapdoor of the longjohns. The old man let out a yell that could be heard for miles and pulled both triggers—the full blast of both barrels went right through the chicken house door.

After the beller of the blast died down and the smoke cleared away, the family got to looking over the situation. There in the chicken coop were about forty of the prize hens blasted to Kingdom Come.

Mrs. Maggie Sullivan with her chickens.

Everything but a Match

In the late 1800's there was great publicity to lure homesteaders to the wide open spaces of Montana. Many jumped at the chance for free land, but few realized what would be in store for them and came unprepared for the totally different way of life.

To some, this new life on the frontier was to bring difficulties and hardship; to others it was to bring tragedy.

During the height of land grabbing, two young sisters from the East filed on adjoining homesteads in eastern Montana. They had a cabin built which crossed the joint property line so they could be together for company and safety while they proved up their claims.

As winter approached, they arrived at the railhead of the closest town and hired a freighter to move all of their worldly goods and supplies, as they had no transportation of their own.

It was starting to turn very cold as the horses pulled up to the cabin door. Hurriedly the driver unloaded the wagon and helped move everything inside.

The sisters assured him that they had everything they needed to be comfortable, so he did not tarry, as the approaching storm threatened a blizzard, and this was no country to be caught out in during a storm.

Several days passed before the storm abated, and the freighter, feeling a sense of concern, drove to the cabin. As he pulled up he called out, announcing his arrival. After receiving no acknowledgement to his call, nor any answer to his knock, he pushed open the door to find the two sisters under a pile of blankets, coats, rugs, and anything else they could find to keep out the cold.

There they lay wrapped in each others' arms—frozen to death. They had everything they needed except a match to start a fire.

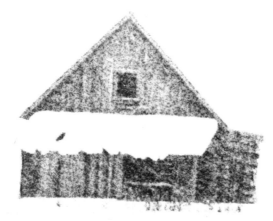

A Close Call

Bill Newell homesteaded 160 acres along Horseshoe Creek in the shadow of Wyoming's Laramie Mountains. By the late 1800's he had built up a herd of Shorthorn cattle that included some of finest in the country.

This particular year, the spring grass was really coming on when a freak April storm hit which left a three foot blanket of white over the entire ranch country. Knowing that the cattle were suffering from the cold and lack of feed, Bill mounted his saddle horse and started out across the plain as soon as the blizzard let up, looking for his main herd. The snow was so deep that the horse was barely able to travel and finally fell exhausted, too tired to go on.

Newell left the pony and plowed through the drifts on foot until he reached a log pen with stacked hay. The cattle were there but unable to reach the feed buried under the pile of snow. By the time he had shoveled the snow away and fed the cattle, he was plumb wore out, but decided it would be easier walking back because of the track he had already broken. To his dismay a light wind had come up and drifted the fine snow over his tracks so he could barely see the route back. It was all he could do to force his way back through the deep drifts.

Nearing exhaustion, he had to stop for longer and longer intervals, each time lying in the snow to catch his breath. Soon he was wet with perspiration and chilled to the bone by the cold wind. At last he fell into a drift and knew he could go no farther.

Through the growing darkness he could barely see a band of horses standing out of the deep snow on a ridge a quarter mile away. He could tell the horses had seen him, but he knew he didn't have a chance to reach them. Just out of curiosity, the horses wallowed through the snow to his side. Picking out a sturdy, short-legged work horse that was gentle but had never been ridden, Newell grabbed him by the mane and managed to get astride. The rugged animal waded through the deep drifts in the darkness while the others followed, with unerring instinct, taking Newell back towards the safety of home.

All that he remembered was the sleighbell-like sound of the icicles hanging from the horses, jingling together in the still of the cold night air.

Everlasting Lessons

Camas Prairie, on Idaho's Salmon River breaks, was a pretty wild place when Grandpa Bruner moved his family there in the early 1880's. After spending the summer and fall getting the homestead built, it was time to prepare for the winter work.

There wasn't much chance for formal book learning, as school was usually held only during the summer months. Much of a child's education was by actual experience. It was no different for young Ralph Bruner, when he joined his father and neighbors to cut logs to split into rails for fences. It was a long way to the mountains, so the group stayed in a small cabin while they were felling trees and hauling the logs out by sled. The younger boys helped where they could and invariably learned something in the process.

One day Ralph and his brother Willie were splitting rails when they found a log too large for the wedges. Being inventive young lads, they decided that black powder would be just the ticket to do the job since they had seen this used by their fathers. After they bored a hole in the log, they couldn't find any powder, so Willie substituted a stick of dynamite, put it in the hole, and lit the fuse. The log didn't gently split as they had expected, but blew clean in half and crosswide, sending a piece about the size of a man's leg over their heads and clear through the cabin wall. Luckily the two escaped any harm, but they sure learned a lesson they never forgot.

Another day young Ralph was helping his father some distance from the camp. On the way back to the cabin, they discovered they had left the axe behind. It was growing cold and dark, but young Ralph was sent back for it. By the time he found the axe, the last bit of daylight was gone and he lost no time in trying to catch up with the loaded sled. As he hurried along, he thought he heard something behind him, and looking over his shoulder he saw the outline and glistening eyes of a cougar.

His first thought was to throw the axe and run—but then he remembered men telling that, unless excited, mountain lions were not apt to attack, but if he were to run, the big cat might pounce. He prayed that the cat was following only out of curiosity and not from pangs of hunger!

So, with heart pounding, he continued down the skid road, hoping at every turn that he would see his father's sled. Imagine what it would have been like, traveling that half-mile or so in darkness, being tracked by a wild creature that weighed more than you. It must have seemed like an eternity. At last the jingle of sleigh bells drifted through the cold night air. Then he heard the horses hoofs on the frozen ground along with the creak of sled runners in the snow. Seeing the sled ahead, he yelled, made a quick dash, and clambered to the top of the load, safe from the marauding cat.

The cougar then silently returned to the shadow of the forest after impressing a young lad with a most unforgettable experience in the wild.

The Threat of Wolves

In the early 1900's longhorn steers still roamed the rolling prairie of eastern Wyoming and threatened to raise havoc with any fence built around their favorite watering holes.

In March of 1913, Edgar and Adaline Wynecoop filed on a 320-acre homestead about fifteen miles north of Gillette. They hired a carpenter and built a story-and-a-half house, a spacious structure compared to the shacks which were constructed for the bachelors and maiden ladies. Fences around the place were a necessity in order to keep the stock away from the buildings, garden, and spring.

One December day, Edgar headed north to cut cedar posts from the forest about ten miles from the homestead. As evening approached, his two-year-old daughter, Altamae, was standing at the double windows watching for her father's return. Suddenly, a large grey wolf appeared in the light shining from the lamp in the room. He stopped within a few feet of the window, staring in.

Altamae let out a cry, "Coyote, Mama, coyote."

Her mother came running and had a good look at the animal before he turned and vanished into the dusk. No tracks remained, as the ground was bare of snow, but she knew from its size that it surely was no coyote.

A few days later, on a ridge a half-mile away, the family watched as a wolf pack hunted a small bunch of longhorns. They herded together as a wolf pack circled and worried the steers. Frequently, one of the wolves would dart in, looking for a leghold, in an attempt to hamstring the critter. The wolves continued circling until one of the longhorns finally broke away with the others following behind. The pack took chase until they overtook the last animal and surrounded him. He courageously stood at bay, tossing his four foot length of horns at any wolf that came close. Suddenly he made a desperate break to catch up with the others. With speed greater than the steer, a large wolf lunged for his hind legs, took a firm hold, held on, and brought the steer to a stop.

Two others rushed in and went for the throat. The great horns thrashed from side to side to keep them away. A fourth wolf circled and grabbed the steer's other back leg just above the hock. The big steer fell and left his throat exposed. It was over quickly.

Turned Away

John McCubbin had moved his family to the Wallowa Valley of eastern Oregon in 1878. Just the previous year, the homesteaders fled the valley during the Nez Perce War, even though Chief Joseph promised that no harm would ever come to them from his tribe.

After Joseph's surrender at Bear Paw Mountain in northern Montana in the fall of 1877, the pioneers returned to their homes, with about 75 new settlers coming with them. Throughout the winter and spring, the newcomers were busy locating their homesteads and cutting logs for cabins.

All around the valley land was being cleared, fences constructed, and ground broken for planting crops. It seemed there was one house-raising party after another, with the men bringing their tools and the women packing lunches, with plans to visit while the cabins were being built.

All was not quiet and peaceful though, for from time to time there came rumors telling of difficulties and friction between the settlers and the Bannock-Paiute Indians who lived in southern Idaho and surrounding areas. Although they were miles away, there was always the threat that if the Indians went on the warpath they might turn north and attack the little settlement in the Wallowa Valley.

Around the first of May, General Howard of the U.S. Army sent a messenger to the valley to warn the settlers that the Indians were expected to go on the warpath and that they should prepare to defend themselves. It was believed that there were now enough men in the valley to protect the settlement if they were properly prepared. Everyone immediately went to work to build makeshift forts on Alderslope, Prairie Creek, and the Richardson Ranch. It seemed that the Richardson place, in the middle of the valley, was the best for defense since it was on open ground where there were no trees or brush around to conceal the Indians should they attack. The Richardson stockade was built double-walled with two lines of posts about fifteen inches apart, filled with dirt to the height of a man's shoulders, and portholes for shooting through cut just above the dirt line. As another precaution, a volunteer company was organized to guard the mountain passes that led into the southern part of the valley.

Just as things looked secure for the settlers, an even greater threat arose with the spread of diptheria to the children of the Walla Walla and Wallowa valleys. First to die was Allie McNalls, followed by Susan Sturgel. Then a family who camped on Parsnip Creek lost two.

All were warned to stay away from anyone who was sick. But the Findley brothers were out riding for cattle when they passed the Parsnip Creek camp. The family had already left, and the boys did not get off their horses; there must have been some germs in the air, for the oldest brother contracted the disease on the sixth of July. Two days later a messenger for General Howard brought news that the Indians had gone on the warpath and they were headed for Wallowa Valley. Everyone was warned to take refuge in the forts.

No one knew just how long they would be holed up in the stockades, so, without delay, John McCubbin headed to Walla Walla for supplies. His wife, Marietta, was not allowed entry to the fort for she had a sick child and the people inside feared it was diptheria. So, she returned home alone to stay with her children.

The local Nez Perces kept close watch on them, bringing them meat which they placed on a stump in the front yard. Many times they were seen staring in through the windows. But, while everyone else was scared to death, no harm came to Marietta or the children, for she and her husband had always welcomed the Indians to their homestead.

Skirmishes

Plains Indian.

It was inevitable that the white man's invasion of the Western frontier would bring conflict. At first only small numbers of settlers trespassed the Indian's land, but soon there were great wagon trains and livestock by the thousands traveling the routes westward. Timber and grass disappeared along the trails, white man's diseases spread, and the great buffalo herds were vanishing. It's little wonder that the Indians became upset about the onslaught on their land.

Montana manhunters of the 1870's.

White man's greed caused continuing conflicts. There was increasing demand for land and riches as many searched for the easy life, wishing not to expend a fair days work. Claims were jumped. Highwaymen stopped stages carrying gold and affluent passengers. Except for vigilantes, the only law was the military stationed at outlying army posts.

Union Pacific Railroad construction in 1866.

The power barons knew no limits to satisfying their greed for the land, riches, and control. Railroads steamed westward, gobbling up the land and timber while running roughshod over anyone or anything in their path. The great buffalo herds were doomed forevermore.

Indian Camp at Pine Ridge, Nebraska in 1891.

The cattlemen drove out the dirt farmer, and then fought with the sheepmen. Outlaws, rustlers, and horse thieves roamed the land looking for easy pickings. Treaties were broken. More land was taken. Outright war was declared against the Indian Nations. The red man was pushed back or confined to reservations. The Indian ways were no more.

It Pays to be Short

It was 1863 when James Allison enlisted as a drummer boy in the Seventeenth Kentucky Regiment commanded by his father. At the age of fourteen he was the second youngest man on the northern side during the war between the States.

The harshness of the Civil War caused many privations on all of the soldiers—long marches, insufficient food, inadequate sleep—but being so young, it seemed to affect Allison more than most. The Army doctors told him he should have been a six-footer. As it was, he was only five feet, two inches tall, causing him to be known as *Shorty* by his fellow soldiers.

On one occasion, his short stature probably saved his life. The Union troops were marching into action with the drummer boys at the head of the column with the flag bearers. Allison was right at the front, followed by another drummer who was well over six feet tall. As the column marched to the roll of the drums, a rifle cracked and a minie ball wizzed over Allison's head, striking the drummer behind him squarely in the forehead—killing him instantly.

Shorty Allison survived the war years and continued on through West Point; he retired as a Brigadier General after seeing service on the Indian frontier.

Devil Horse

After graduating from West Point, Lt. James Allison's first assignment was with the Second Calvary at old Fort Laramie on the North Fork of Wyoming's Platte River.

Shortly after arriving at the fort, he walked into the stables and came upon the most magnificient black horse he had ever seen—standing there a full seventeen hands high. A stable hand noted his interest and told him that this was a devil horse called Satan, who had already killed two men who had tried to ride him.

Allison could not take his eyes off the horse—it was such a beautiful mount. Right then and there he decided, come what might, he had to have that horse. He didn't waste any time getting to headquarters to ask for the horse to be assigned to him. With considerable misgivings, his troop commander granted his request.

Inquiring further, he found that the two men had been killed in exactly the same manner—the horse had bolted with them and then thrown them into a stone watering trough just outside the stable.

Lt. Allison put on a pair of sharp spurs, and with two men holding the horse, swung up in the saddle. As soon as the horse was free of their grip, he took the bit in his teeth and bolted—straight for the watering trough. Just as he got there, Allison lifted him with the reins and drove the spurs home. Instead of refusing as he had before, Satan sailed over the trough like a bird and headed straight for the prairie on a dead run.

On and on he ran. When he began to tire and slow his gait, the spurs were driven home again. Once more the horse and rider were at breakneck speed. Every time the horse tried to slacken gait, those spurs went home again. When the horse began to stagger and was scarcely able to go on, Lt. Allison finally let up and returned to the fort with Satan gently walking.

From then on the two were inseparable. In their first battle together which was a hand-to-hand affair, they were opposed by an Indian on a pony. The young brave made a slash with his tomahawk. Lt. Allison counter guarded with his saber, but the tomahawk glanced off and cut a long gash in Satan's haunch. It was something he never forgot. From that day on, whenever they went into battle together, Satan would scream like the devil, rear up, and strike—taking both Indian and pony down under his hoofs. Lt. Allison never had to use his saber again in close combat.

Savage Justice

The wagon train of pioneers and gold seekers left Independence, Missouri in the spring of 1850, headed for northern California. The time passed uneventfully for several weeks until they were well into Indian Territory. One evening, after Captain Ira Fassett had formed the wagons in a circle, half a dozen men rode out in search of fresh meat. One rider veered off from the others, weaving his horse quietly through the brush and into a clump of small trees. Coming out into a small rise, he gazed across the landscape, and in the dim light he saw what looked like a doe drinking from a water hole. Not wishing to chance scaring the animal off, he drew a quick bead and fired his rifle. When he rode closer his heart leaped into his throat. He had killed an Indian squaw dipping water from the stream. Frightened, he wheeled his horse around and raced back to the wagon train.

Some hours later, a small band of Indians, tight-lipped and fierce-looking, rode slowly up to the circle of wagons and halted. The leader kicked his pony a few steps forward. His reddish-brown skin glistened in the light of the campfire. He looked down at the pioneers gathered around him and made signs indicating that he wanted to talk to their leader. In a few minutes Captain Fassett stood before the Indian. After much sign language and guttural sounds from both sides, Fassett realized that the tall Indian mounted before him was the Chief and he wanted to punish the man who had killed his squaw. Fassett refused to hand him over, whereupon the Indian, again through signs and grunts, let it be known that if the man was not given to them he would return with many braves, burn the wagons, and kill them all.

Captain Fassett was a cautious man. He asked for time to consider the Chief's request. The Indians withdrew a short distance and waited ominously.

It took the Captain but a few minutes to identify the guilty man, who, of course, protested loudly against being handed over to the Indians. Some of the other men sided with him. When a heated argument resolved nothing, Fassett selected a six-man committee to settle the question. Another argument began among the committee members, but soon enough they realized they had no choice. In the end, the entire committee decided that the good of the wagon train came before any individual in it.

The accused man became violent when he heard the committee's decision and had to be subdued by four men. They tied him and dragged him, feet first, to the Indians. Captain Fassett looked up into the black eyes of the Chief. "Take him," he said sternly, hoping to make an end to it.

But the Indians had other ideas. They told the Captain they wanted four white men to ride with them into the woods and see justice done. Fassett was not willing to consent to this, but when the chief threatened to annihilate the entire wagon train, Fassett and three of his group mounted up and rode out with the Indians.

The party stopped in a clearing several miles away, where the Indians tied the man to a tree and stripped off his clothes while others built a fire. Then, with knives heated in the fire, two braves mutilated their prisoner. The four white men watched the victim writhe in agony and scream from the pain, but they dared not move to help him.

Strips of metal were placed in the fire until they glowed. These were pressed against the man's body, covering it with red welts. The Indians danced about and shrieked with joy each time their victim screamed in pain. Horrible sounds issued from his throat as the torture continued. All Fassett and his men could do was to stare in horror.

Then the Indians formed a line. One by one they approached the crazed man with knives drawn. Each in turn cut loose a patch of flesh at the shoulder or upper chest and ripped it down in quick movements, each Indian grunting in his effort to pull off a longer strip than the brave who had preceded him.

Within a few minutes the excruciating pain killed the white man, and the Indians, satisfied at last, untied the victim and dropped him at the feet of the four white men. Then they mounted their ponies and rode off into the darkness. Indian justice was done.

Fassett and the others buried their former companion on the spot and themselves returned to the wagon train, too drained emotionally to speak. The next morning the wagons moved westward again, in peace.

A Charmed Life

Walter Braten was probably one of the youngest pioneers to leave his family behind and head West alone. In the spring of 1869, at the tender age of ten, he left McComb, Michigan to join a group of freighters in Sioux City, Iowa. They were headed for Indian country in the Dakotas, and Walter was going with them, determined to seek his fortune in the western territories.

As the wagons neared Diamond Springs in the Dakotas, Indians appeared in full war dress, much to the thrill and delight of the ten-year-old boy. The braves, decorated in war paint and feathers, were soon routed by the men in the wagon train, only to reappear by nightfall. Though the men kept careful vigilance during the night, they relaxed their guard toward morning, opening the way for Indian attack and massacre of every adult in the wagon train. Only Walter, who was sleeping in one of the wagons and hidden by piles of sacked flour, escaped the onslaught of the enraged Indians.

Thus, he fell captive to the Brule Indians who took him to Wolf Creek, 300 miles west of the Missouri River. There Chief Standing Bear, of the Oglala Sioux, adopted him as a son, naming him Young Standing Bear. He soon learned the Indian ways and became one of them in every sense of the word.

It was five years that he roamed with the Indian Nations before he was able to escape and make his way to a white settlement in western Nebraska. Not long afterward he became a scout for General Custer and the 7th Calvary Regiment, joining the march to the Little Bighorn in 1876. But, as luck would have it, the young scout came down with typhoid fever and was left at the government hospital at Ft. Pierre on the Missouri. Once again fate played a crucial role in his life, for Custer and all two hundred of his troopers were massacred by the Indians. Only Comanche, Captain Myles Keogh's gelding horse, survived the Indian attack at the Battle of the Little Bighorn.

Shoshone Indians in the Wind River area of Wyoming.

Prisoner of War

The battle of the Little Bighorn was the U.S. Army's most decisive defeat during the Indian wars, but it also sealed the fate of the Indian Nations. After the death of Custer and his men at the Battle of the Little Bighorn the national mood hardened; whatever chances there were for men of goodwill to bridge the gaps between Indians and white men were lost. Government officials and military leaders could only address themselves to one task—crush the Indian resistance once and for all.

General George Crook was the first to attempt sweet revenge. In August of '76 he ordered his men to abandon all wagons, tents, and extra clothes in the interest of speed in pursuing a well-mounted force of Sioux.

Traveling light, Crook expected to catch the savages within a few days. But the chase continued for weeks, through Wyoming into Montana and east to the Dakota Territory. Fall weather came early with rain, sleet, and hail.

By early September the Sioux had turned south into the Badlands, leaving the soldiers far behind with no supplies, suffering from hunger, frostbite, and rheumatism. Soon the troops ran out of supplies entirely and resorted to killing their mounts for food. All Crook could do was to seek relief and supplies, for his men were in no shape to continue the long pursuit.

Colonel Nelson Miles took up a midwinter campaign against the Sioux. In fanatical pursuit, he dressed his men in buffalo coats and marched them two hundred miles in temperatures reaching to 50 degrees below zero. The hardships were incredible. At breakfast the troops were huddled around white-hot stoves in their Sibley tents, their food still froze to the plates!

Col. Nelson Miles and staff — the winter of 1876.

The Indians could not conceive of any threat from the Calvary under such weather conditions, so they had no sentries out. Their village was taken completely by surprise as the calvary charged. The Indians poured out of their teepees, men and women grabbing up what weapons they could. The troops had no chance to discriminate between the sexes. There was a brief, violent action and Sioux were scattered, their horses captured, and their power broken.

After the skirmish, a young Indian girl was found hiding in a creek bed. She had gotten a pistol ball through the fleshy part of her forearm. Despite her wound she fought like a wildcat as she was brought in. As the Army surgeon dressed her wound, she stood there—no wimper, no sound. She asked a question in the Sioux language. The interpreter translated her question as, "when the torture was to begin." That was the Indian way; she could not comprehend anything different.

She was held captive while her wound was healing, but she refused to eat. After two days of hunger fast, Lt. James Allison ordered her brought to his tent. When she came in, he motioned her to sit down. At the table next to her was a dish of stewed peaches which he had prepared. He sat at his table across the tent busily writing and watching her out of the corner of his eye. She sat looking at him, then her gaze wandered to the peaches. She looked at him again, then one finger stole out, dipped into the peaches, and then into her mouth. Then she grabbed the dish and bolted the contents like a wild animal. Her hunger strike was broken. When her wound was healed, she was released and immediately returned to the safety of her tribe.

A Plan Gone Awry

The westbound passenger train,
carrying mail and express, chugged up the
Blue Mountains grade the second day of July, 1914.

The Portland-Chicago Special

At Kamela station, the train slowed to a stop to detach the helper engine.

Three men boarded the back of the tender as the train pulled out. They climbed over the coal and into the engine cab where they forced the engineer at gun point to bring the train to a stop. The engineer and the fireman were taken back to the baggage car, where they were lined up with the rest of the crew, facing the wall and guarded by one of the robbers. The other two quickly searched the express car but found the loot was disappointing so they decided to rob the passengers.

Upon entering the first coach, one of the robbers halted at the entrance holding his gun on the passengers, while the other went down the aisle collecting money, watches, and jewelry in a small canvas bag. As soon as he finished, he took over guarding the passengers while the first man made his way through the car—then both backed out, facing their victims.

After robbing the second coach they became careless and, instead of facing their victims, they walked out with their backs to them. It only took a split second for George McDuffy, a deputy sheriff from Heppner, to draw his gun and fire. In the lively exchange of shots the deputy was wounded and one robber was killed.

The other one picked up the bag of loot and ran back to the baggage car to gather up the guard robber, then both fled through the timber toward the highway that paralleled the railroad. It was thought that they made their getaway by automobile; roadblocks were set in place, but the robbers never showed up.

Locomotive engineer Jacobson had a couple of trained bloodhounds which he brought up from La Grande. No law officers had shown up yet, so Jacobson and Ed Wetzel, with hounds on leash, started up the hill after the bandits. They were sure they would lose the trail when they reached the highway, but the dogs picked up the scent, crossed the road, and headed for the timber. Neither man felt very easy about chasing armed robbers through the forest, so they turned the dogs loose, thinking they would be a ways behind when the robbers were brought to bay.

The hounds traveled less than a mile when they started wandering in circles and sneezing. Jacobson and Wetzel suspected that pepper had been placed on the trail. They felt somewhat relieved that the robbers had gotten away, as they leashed the hounds and backtracked to the scene of the crime where a large crowd of armed men had gathered.

It was now known that the fugitives were on foot and the direction they were traveling. A posse went back with the dogs, creating one of the most sensational manhunts in Northwest history up to that time. But their luck was no better than on the first effort; the search was finally abandoned, but guards were placed on all trails and roads leading out of the mountains. Every train was stopped coming and going, searches were made, and hobos were taken off and questioned, but the fugitives evidently disappeared into thin air.

But hunger finally turned the tide. After a couple of weeks, two men and a sheep dog showed up at Hilgard to purchase food and supplies— stepping right into the arms of the law. After a long grilling, the two confessed and led the sheriff to the cache of loot.

The robber who was killed was thought to be an elusive outlaw named Whitney, because that was the name engraved on the back pocket watch removed from his body. But the two men in custody said their leader's name was Charles Manning of Cokeville, Wyoming. He was a friend of Whitney. The watch had been won in a poker game.

The two accomplices, Albert Meadows and Clarence Stoner, had been sheepherders in Idaho when they were invited by Manning to go along with him on the train robbery.

The crime had been well planned, as they had laid in a stock of food and supplies in a canyon hideout. Their scheme had been to lay low after the robbery until the heat was off, when they could have left the country.

The trick with the pepper had worked to perfection, but the food supply played out far too soon.

This was Meadow's and Stoner's first robbery, and their last for a number of years, because their new home was the State Penitentiary.

On the Move

Wagon train and oxen in the Blue Mountains.

The pioneer wagons opened the first roads westward. As settlement increased, so did the demand for more routes and better transportation. Freight wagons replaced the pack mules for hauling supplies from the waterways to the towns and the mines.

The Baker-Prairie City Stage at Austin House.

Stagecoaches became the order of the day to move passengers more comfortably and gold more safely. The Butterfield Stages, Hollady Lines, and Wells Fargo Express networked the West.

Steamboats on the Snake River at Lewistown, Idaho.

Steamboats plied the rivers, carrying cargo and settlers upstream from more civilized points. Military personnel and supplies moved from fort to fort along the waterways. Furs, hides, and disillusioned travelers were aboard for the return trip to more civilized places.

The Sumpter Valley Railroad.

The completion of the transcontinental railroads brought about the demise of the freighters and the stagelines. A new era was born in moving passengers and goods across the country.

Vacationing in the California Redwoods.

The horse and buggy was still in vogue and would remain a principal means of transportation for a few decades yet to come.

Motor Cars in Richland, Oregon.

The development of a new-fangled contraption called a motor car, along with surfaced roadways, revolutionized transportation and made the horse obsolete in getting from town to town.

A Reluctant Move

Mamie Jones was a city gal at heart. She liked all of the conveniences, comforts, and fineries of the big town, but she fell in love with a horseman. Now George Hastings made his living breaking horses—and Mamie hated horses, but not enough to give up George.

While they were courting, she swore up and down that he never took her for a buggy ride with tame horses. It seems that there was always a critter under harness being broke in—turning a quiet afternoon buggy ride into a *ride of your life* or an outright runaway.

Besides hating horses, she didn't care one iota about the Western Frontier. But George could see great opportunities and he did have a persuasive manner about him. When he asked Mamie to go with him as his wife, she finally consented, but under one condition — only if the trip was not under horse power.

It was a long train ride to the Siskiyou Mountains of southern Oregon in the late 1800's. At Jump Off Joe Creek they transferred their meager belongings to a buckboard, right in the middle of a pouring-down rainstorm. The ride up to Quartz Creek was in the dead of night. All along the way they could hear the water rushing wildly in the streams — and it was all that George could do to get the team and wagon across the stream in the height of the storm.

As they pulled up to a cabin, Mamie was appalled at the sight. George's Uncle Alf was a dyed-in-the-heart mountain man, and his cabin looked it — hardly the neat and clean conditions she was used to. On top of that she was scared to death that there were savages lurking behind every tree.

George went out looking for his uncle while Mamie dried out, unpacked, and started to straighten things around.

All of a sudden she heard ahootin' and ahollerin' and thought the savages were attacking just as George burst through the doorway, screaming for her washtubs. Now those tubs were about the last bit of civilization that she still had — and George thought he was going to have to wrestle her for them.

She finally gave in — completely baffled as to what was going on. Without a word of explanation, George just grabbed the tubs and ran, for time was awastin' — forty-pound salmon were running in the creek and they just wouldn't be there forever.

She had too much spirit to let herself be completely *broke in* to his every whim; after this incident she accepted the fact that in order to be happy in her man's world she would have to compromise — at least once in awhile.

Lost in a Blizzard

Hundreds of geese could be heard faintly honking their way southward from the Milk River. There seemed to be an urgency to this mass migration. The silhouette of rigid V formations moved swifty across the brilliant full moon, as if they were being driven ahead by an unseen force. Likely there was a storm in the air.

Ed Wetzel was having a great time visiting his brother, Sid, on the Montana border ranch, but he figured he better head back to Oregon before the weather changed.

The following morning, the two hitched up the team and got an early start. A storm was brewing out of the north and it was spitting a little snow by the time they reached town. Ed took one look at the sky and warned his brother that he better stay at the hotel overnight and not chance getting caught in a blizzard. But, as soon as Ed left on the afternoon train, Sid figured that he could reach home before the storm hit.

He started the team out on the main trail heading for the ranch. The prairie land was flat for miles, with no fences since this was all a grazing reserve. Before Sid was two miles out with the team and wagon, the blizzard hit in all its fury. Visibility was zero. The air was full of wind-driven, blinding snow, and it was bitter cold.

After a short time it seemed that the wagon was bumping across badger holes. Sid stopped the horses, got off, made a narrow circle around the wagon, and found he was on the open prairie. He dared not get away from the wagon more than a few feet for fear of not being able to find it again.

He climbed back aboard and gave the horses their heads, hoping their sense of direction would take them home. Instead, they were drifting south with the storm. After a bit, the wagon jolted badly, as if crossing a rutted wagon road. Sid knew this had to be the Boundary Trail. The roaring blizzard chilled him to the bone, and he knew if he didn't find shelter soon, he surely would perish in the storm.

He swung the team into the Boundary Trail, which the horses followed until they reached a fenced lane—one that Sid recognized as leading to his home and shelter. He was nearly frozen, especially his ears, hands, and feet, but he was safe.

Sid realized that his poor judgement had nearly cost him his life out on that cold vast plain. Right then and there he vowed he would never be that foolish again.

The Rawhide Railroad

Dorsey Baker knew how he was going to make his fortune on the frontier. The powerful railroad magnates were pushing westward, but there was nothing to any extent in the Northwest as yet.

Transportation to move supplies from the Columbia ports inland was at a premium. Everything moving to the settlements and the mines was by pack train and freight wagon, so Baker conceived the idea of building a railroad from Wallula on the Columbia River, east to the town of Walla Walla.

Even though it was the first railroad in the Northwest, outside of the short portage lines around Cascade Rapids and Celilo Falls, it was a complete bust the first year. The shipment of rails from England was not enough to complete the job and he was forced to use wooden rails on some of the track. Rawhide strips were nailed on top and across the joints to hold the rails in place, so his project was promptly dubbed 'The Rawhide Railroad'. His ingenuity would have worked, too, except for the fact that the next winter was a harsh one and hungry coyotes chewed off and ate most of the rawhide.

It wasn't until the second year, when another bunch of rails and a narrow-gauge Pony Locomotive were shipped around the Horn and up the Columbia by clipper ship, then transferred to a river boat for the final journey up the river, that Dorsey Baker fulfilled his dream.

While everyone else was seeking their fortunes in gold dust and cattle, Baker made his charging high rates for passengers and freight traveling the thirty miles from the river to town. Then he added to his wealth when he sold out to the Northern Pacific as they built westward over the mountains and reached Walla Walla.

Cherokee Run

After years of pressure by western Congressmen, railroad lobbyists, and *Boomer* spokesmen, Congress finally relented to establishing the Oklahoma Territory in 1890. Over the next couple of years reservation land of the Sauk, Fox, Potewatomi, and the Cheyenne-Arapaho was opened to white settlement. But the most dramatic rush was set for September 16, 1893.

On that fateful morning, 100,000 landseekers waited eagerly for the noon opening to 6,000,000 acres called the Cherokee Strip. For miles on end horsemen, wagons, hacks, carriages, buckboards, and a host of other vehicles defying description stood wheel to wheel awaiting the noontime signal for the rush. Army troops were stationed at regular intervals to hold back *sooners* unwilling to await the deadline.

As synchronized watches ticked off the minutes, officers waited with guns in the air, ready to signal the opening. At noon a string of shots rang out and pandemonium broke out all along the line—riders whipped their horses, wagons careened wildy foreward, horses galloped away from overturned vehicles—all was excitement and hurrah!

In the middle of the melee were Winfield Scott Hastings and his wife, Elizabeth. They had to overcome a small problem as she was part Indian, and Indians could not homestead free land. They destroyed her papers.

The couple had left their children in a covered wagon, their only home for several years, and picked their two fastest horses for the land rush. Winfield and Elizabeth had previously spotted a couple of choice parcels, so with their spirited horses, they had no trouble staking a claim to the land—a section apiece to homestead, raise their family, and plant corn that would grow as high as a mule's eye.

The family had lived out of a covered wagon for so long that they just weren't used to neighbors. They intentionally picked a spot so that no one else was within miles. Finally, to the relief of the children, they were settling down to a permanent home. The crops were in and they were enjoying life. But then someone settled about 20 miles away. That was just too close for Winfield Scott Hastings. He traded the land for some mules, horses, and two wagons, gathered his family, and pulled up stakes for more unsettled territory.

Too Much Speed

It was the winter of 1910 and Ed Wetzel had just taken a job as signal master for the Oregon-Washington Railroad and Navigation Company at Huron in the Blue Mountains of northeast Oregon.

One Sunday while he was working, a lone engine came through, running fast — too fast for the engineer to grab for the train-order hoop. He didn't get stopped until the old steamer was nearly to the west switch. The engineer backed to pick up the order, then opened the throttle wide and tore out of sight at a speed that was nothing but reckless for the crooked track winding down through Meacham Canyon.

Frank Woughter, the telegraph operator remarked, "They may have to fish him out of the creek down the line somewhere."

Later, Woughter heard over the wire that at the foot of Cayuse Hill, the locomotive had failed to make a sharp curve and had turned partly over up against a bank. The Umatilla River was to the right and quite a ways below the tracks, but the locomotive and tender had tipped to the left. Evidently the high speed, coupled with the centrifugal force, caused the locomotive to tilt in this position. Since the wheels were off the track, the protective block signals indicated *proceed* to other traffic on the line.

The engineer on an approaching westbound freight could not see the obstruction until too close to do more than shout a quick warning to the fireman, close the throttle, apply the air, and jump to safety. The locomotive and a dozen or so freight cars crashed and tumbled into the river.

When a crew reached the wreck they found the cab of the lone engine partly filled with coal that had catapulted out of the tender. Under the pile of coal, up against the firebox, were the bodies of the engineer and fireman.

This was supposed to have been the last run for the fireman as a bachelor since he planned to be married when he came in from the trip.

Instead of a wedding, it was a funeral.

California, Here We Come!

John Bruner hated to give up, but there had been too many dry years and wheat farming was no longer a profitable business for him, so he decided to give up his farm at Kahlotus on Washington's Snake River breaks and move his family to Los Angeles.

The family packed their 1921 Model-T Ford open touring car with all of their belongings and headed south in the summer of 1923.

It was a sight to behold—suitcases, boxes, bedding, and camping equipment strapped to the outside of the car with mother, father, four children, and their cello and violins squeezed together on the inside. Fastened to the driver's side was Mother Bruner's pride and joy, a tin fruit dryer which served as a cupboard for the dishes, pots, pans, and groceries for the trip.

Although both parents were of hardy pioneer stock and had experienced adventures in the covered wagon days, this journey was rather frightening to them, with thoughts of leaving their home and roots behind and venturing into an unknown future, with the responsibility of four children to keep happy and healthy.

The first few days were spent driving through the beautiful gorges and mountains of Washington and Oregon, high above the picturesque streams and rivers. There was certainly ample time for the family to enjoy the new scenery, as the little car, so heavily overloaded, did not travel very fast.

And there were the hazards to contend with—narrow, rough and crooked roads, steep dropoffs, and grades into canyons that seemed to have no bottom—all of this with no safety brakes.

Money was scarce; there were no warm motels to rest in, and no restaurants to greet the family when they were hungry. It was an ordeal to keep the younger children sitting quiet on such a long journey, as they had so little room to move around in, especially since they were used to the wide open spaces of the farm. They soon learned to keep occupied by counting birds, railroad cars, livestock, and anything else in numbers.

John Bruner was always nervous when he drove a car, and many times said that he felt much safer behind the team of horses he had driven for years. His wife, Mary, didn't really trust the modern mode of travel and spent much of her time making suggestions to her husband regarding the driving, which probably didn't help his nerves much. He was especially bad on sharp curving roads, scaring himself and all the kids; his wife was petrified. Quite often Mother Bruner would get out and walk ahead to be sure that it was safe for the little car carrying her precious load. On the worst occasions her husband would stop the car to quiet everyone down, ease his nerves, and then turn the wheel over to their eighteen-year-old daughter, Pearl.

The most dangerous curves in their travels were posted with a sign that read, "Blow your horn before approaching!" These signs were always the cue for Mother Bruner to get out and walk ahead.

Sometimes the car would just refuse to go—it would just stop, steam, and boil. One of the family would add water from the canvas bag that hung on the side of the car, then all the passengers would walk along beside the car until it regained its strength.

One day they came to a very long hill—the Hornbrook Grade—a steep pull dreaded by travelers of that time. Many cars were at the foot of the grade—some were turning back, and others were resting for the long climb—it was steep going up for 2½ miles followed by a steep descent for 5 miles on the other side of the mountain. After much discussion with the other travelers, John Bruner decided he would at least give it a try. After many stops, adding water, and the family walking for some stretches, they crawled to the top. There they parked under some big trees and Mother Bruner opened the tin cupboard to fix the family lunch. Again there was discussion as to the safety of going down the other side. It was finally decided that Henry Ford had a long way to go in perfecting the brake system, so a large pine tree was cut and tied to the rear of the car to hold it back—reminiscent of the old days when the same technique was used to slow the covered wagons descending steep grades.

The family followed as the car started down the grade. It was great fun for the younger kids, watching the tree spinning, the branches popping off, and the dust boiling up, punctuated by Mother Bruner's cries of "Watch Out! We'll all be killed!", amid the smell of fast-burning brakes and the sound of a growling motor. The parents' prayers must have been answered for they reached the bottom of the grade safely.

After spending several nights in campgrounds and one night on the beach near the ocean, the family reached Eureka, California. Mother Bruner was sick, the Ford was sputtering, and the family finances were nearly exhausted, so John Bruner decided that the logical thing to do was to stay there until his wife was well again. He went to work in a sawmill and rented a house for the family. They were far short of their destination, but a least they got to California to start life anew.

The Wrangler's Last Ride

Long years ago a family from Wales emmigrated to the West and, in due course of time, built up extensive ranch holdings near Deadwood, South Dakota. They also owned and operated the Bar H Ranch north of Slim Buttes along the South Grand River. There a retired, but by no means decrepit, member of the family, Dave, chose to spend his declining years. But it was not his nature to stay idle for any great length of time, so he spent his days as a sometimes wrangler and stablehand, occasional cook's assistant during branding and roundup, and then general flunky when things were slow. He was especially helpful during the busy season by taking charge of the cook's two small children to allow her more freedom in the kitchen. Because of this willingness to lend a helping hand he was well known and well liked all around the area.

Thus when word was flashed by word of mouth, as there were no telephones there in the early 1900's, that the Grim Reaper had made his calling, and Dave had punctually responded, friends from far and wide speedily assembled. It seemed imperative that the body be transported to his relatives in Deadwood. Since, at that time, in that area, no such thing as an ambulance or hearse existed, the question was....*How?* To further complicate matters, it was in the dead of winter and the weather was bitter cold.

It is not known who conceived the brilliant, but somewhat weird, plan, but the body was dressed in the best clothing available, and then seated in a lifelike position in a straight-backed kitchen chair. Gentle hands anchored the corpse in that position by means of cloth strips torn from a bedsheet. Then the body and chair were moved to an unheated shed. Working in shifts, Dave's friends maintained a wake of sorts throughout the long night.

Come morning and, as expected, *rigor mortis* and the frigid temperature had done their handywork, and the next step of the plan unfolded. An intrepid and kindly rancher offered the use of his vehicle, with himself as driver, to transport the remains to Deadwood. Reverently, Wrangler Dave was carried to the waiting car and seated in the passenger's seat, secured in place by the same bands that bound him in the chair the night before, and they were on their way. The frozen terrain offered no impediment to travel; the passenger maintained an eerie silence while the driver was free to pursue his undisclosed thoughts.

Still, it must have been a relief for him to stop at a service station in Newell for gas. The driver removed himself from the vehicle to stroll about as he exclaimed, "Get the kinks out of my bones!" Meanwhile the attendant filled the gas tank, checked the oil, and turned his attention to the windshield. With eyes upon his work, he addressed a friendly remark or so to the passenger. Getting no response, he glanced up in dismay. The ghastly countenance that met his gaze so unnerved him that, with extreme difficulty, he refrained from dropping his tools and fleeing in horror. Just then the driver sauntered up and explained the bizarre situation in full.

The remainder of the trip passed without incident. The deceased's relatives were contacted, and the corpse duly delivered to the funeral parlor.

Then ensued a thawing period before the body could be straightened sufficiently to be decently *laid out* in a casket. At long last, Wrangler Dave (may his soul rest in peace), took his last ride and was properly interred in the family plot.

Day by Day

Early-day horse tender.

The frontier was alive with activity. Settlers were busy under horsepower to till the soil and plant the crops — all the while worrying about the threat of Indian attack, insect infestation, early freeze, and summer drought.

Mining the Sumpter gold fields of eastern Oregon.

Miners were panning the streams, tunneling the mountains, and washing the soil from the hills. Most were continually disappointed while a few were consistently striking it rich.

Log Sawyers at the Starbuck Camp — Whitney, Oregon.

Sawmills were going full steam and crews were having a tough time meeting the demands for ties at the railroad, timbers at the mines, and boards for the towns and homes.

The Rasmussen Blacksmith Shop in Elgin, Oregon.

Blacksmiths worked night and day to keep things running in the fields, at the mines, in the woods, and around the towns.

Herding cattle in Cherry County, Nebraska.

Cowhands moved the great herds north to the railheads and beyond. The demand for beef was at its peak for supplying the military forts, Indian Agencies, and the Eastern markets.

Turn-of-the-century farm chores.

Women were pretty well restricted to household chores and raising a family. Rare was the opportunity to seek independence or a career in these times.

The Buhler threshing outfit in western Nebraska.

As steam mechanization came to the frontier, more acreage was planted, and crews moved from farm to farm to harvest the crops to feed the nation.

A Most Memorable Fourth

The 4th of July was something special on the Western frontier. It was a time for celebrating patriotism and independence of one's country. And so it was in the Wallowa Mountains of Oregon in the early 1900's.

There was tremendous excitement in the Bue Family cabin that July 3rd morning. Nels Bue was up before daybreak to get the family ready to attend the three-day 4th of July celebration in Wallowa, 16 miles away. The three oldest children were disappointed because they would have to stay behind to milk the cows and feed the stock. But, on the other hand, they were thrilled at the prospect of staying home alone to look after things.

Berenice, at age 11, and her two younger brothers were to spend the days at home doing the work, and then spend the nights with their neighbor, who lived down the road half a mile, and whose husband was leaving with the Bue Family for the celebration.

In spite of being veterans at milking and caring for the cows, it was late before the children finished their chores and got back to the house for breakfast. Berenice was scrambling a dozen eggs as the boys stood by in ravenous anticipation. Just as the eggs reached the proper degree of creaminess, a man walked through the open front door and into the kitchen.

Without a word, he took the pan of eggs off the stove and walked out onto the porch where he sat down and began eating the eggs with the stirring spoon. Berenice watched in dazed amazement. She had seen rough-looking men before, but there was something indefinable about this man that struck terror in her heart, a feeling she had never known before. It wasn't just the bearded face and the tattered clothes. There was something terribly wrong that she could not grasp.

In a few gulps, he wolfed down the entire pan of eggs. The two boys began to cry, so Berenice whispered, "Come on, boys, let's go behind the cellar and pray."

Her heart was pounding wildly, and her voice shook, but big girls were not supposed to be afraid, so silently she prayed, "Please, God, don't let the boys know how scared I am." It was her voice that calmly finished the Lord's Prayer, although it seemed to come far away from someone else.

When they finished the prayer and the boys stopped crying, there was nothing else to do except return to the house, make another breakfast, and get ready to separate the milk.

Their visitor was lying on the porch, sound asleep, with the empty pan beside him. With exaggerated nonchalance, Berenice walked to the porch and picked up the pan. Lying there, the stranger did not seem very formidable and she felt a little foolish at her first reaction.

The rest of that day was a nightmare for the Bue children. The man was around the house all day, but he acted as if he was alone. He paced the floor restlessly, stared for endless periods out of the windows, and never spoke a word. Out on the porch at noon he ate a huge plate of sandwiches and drank directly from the big pitcher of milk that Berenice had placed beside a glass. The children never knew their clock to tick so loudly, nor move its hands so slowly. It seemed that evening would never come so they could finish their work and head for the neighbor's house. But, it finally did. They finished their work as the man sat on the front porch, staring emptily about.

The children sneaked out around the back of the house, down through the pasture, and through the trees, until they reached the neighbor's. Only then did they sigh with relief as they knocked on her door. No one said a word about the visitor, for they did not wish to worry her, and the man would be gone by morning, anyway.

The neighbor was glad to see them and had a fresh huckleberry shortcake made for a bed-time snack. Her cozy lamp-lighted table was truly a comfort after such a disturbing day. But the comfort didn't last long, for as soon as the whipped cream was being ladled over the shortcake, the now-familiar face appeared at the window. The neighbor lady screamed and dropped her spoon.

Berenice got up from her chair, wearily, as if she had lived this way forever, and told her that the man was not dangerous and she would talk with him, as the woman spoke little English. The man met Berenice at the door and spoke the first words he had uttered since he showed up. He said he was hungry, as he had lived on sawdust for a long time, and he wanted food. She asked him to sit down on the porch and proceeded to serve him about six normal servings of shortcake buried in whipped cream.

They left him there on the porch steps, locked the doors, and went upstairs. The neighbor lady was terrified. She was a thin nervous woman who lived in constant grief over having left her native land. There was a telephone in the house, but, as usual, the line was out of order.

When morning came, the visitor was gone. The chores had to be done so the children trudged home. The man was nowhere in sight, but close to noon, he appeared, crawling out of the haystack, just in time to have lunch with the children. Everyone maintained a total silence, but the man acted terribly nervous, pacing back and forth until Berenice felt she had to do something.

"Let's sing," she said to her brothers. They had an organ, and they sang one hymn after another. The visitor, meanwhile, sat down in the rocker, and while he paid no outward attention to the singing, he appeared more quiet and relaxed as the children sang the refrain over and over again, "The winds and the waves they obey Thy will, peace be still, peace be still...."

Milking time came around again, so they had to abandon hypnotizing their guest, but Berenice was smarter this time. She fed him to the point that he ate reluctantly. Then she told him he could sleep in the bed downstairs in the house instead of having to sleep out in the barn. In that way she hoped to keep him away from the neighbor's that night.

That worked. At least he did not follow them there. But when they returned home the next morning he was busy ringing the dead telephone. They plied him with food again, and unbelievingly, he seemed to have reached the saturation point. He was desperately restless, and stared for longer periods up the road.

Right after the noon meal he left the house and walked uncertainly up the road. About a quarter of a mile away he fell, writhed a while, and lay still. Before the children had time to think, a rig came tearing around the bend, stopped, picked the man up, immediately turned around, and disappeared in a cloud of dust. The episode over; it was time to start the evening chores and clean up the house, for their parents would be home that night.

Finally, everything was done. The house was clean, they had run over to tell the neighbor lady that she needn't worry any more, and they were dressed in their finest, awaiting the return of the rest of the family. The three waited patiently for the familiar faces of old Queen and Bell to appear around the bend in the road. As soon as they saw the dust, they ran up the road to greet their folks and get a ride back to the house.

Immediately the three began bombarding their folks with questions about the celebration in town. Their dad said he had a surprise for them, but it would have to wait until dark. That meant only one thing. Fireworks! Their excitement reached the bursting point. The neighbor took off for home to bring his wife back for the festivities, while their mother hurriedly prepared a rare treat of fresh beefsteak with lettuce and tomatoes.

Then their dad said, "But the biggest excitement of all in town was the hunt for a crazy man who had escaped from Pendleton. Men were out hunting everywhere for him. Somebody thought they had seen him near Wallowa, but they couldn't find him."

"A crazy man?" Berenice repeated, a sudden realization striking her. "Why that must have been the man who was here with us while you were gone."

That was the only time in her life that she had seen fear in her father's face — stark, livid fear.

"They were hunting for him?" she asked. By then her two brothers began chattering and telling the story of the celebration there at home with the strange visitor. Berenice thought of the man's hunger, his worn shoes, the empty look in his eyes, and the way he had fallen in the road. She was not familiar with the word *compassion*. All she knew was that she got that same sick feeling inside as she had when she once looked at a killer grizzly bear in a monstrous trap, his shoulder mangled and blood-crusted, with approaching death filming the defiance in his eyes and the sorrow she always felt for wild things wounded unto death.

Suddenly, she wanted to cry. But she bit her lips together and swallowed the big threatening lump.

Big girls don't cry.

Bear Loco

Sometimes running cattle was a problem in bear country. One such instance was in the summer of 1894 when Bill Newell had his cattle in the foothills between Laramie Peak and Horseshoe Creek in southeastern Wyoming. It seemed that every summer an old rogue bear would jump out of the brush and chase his cattle as they came down to the creek for water. This particular summer the old bear managed to catch one of the cows and kill her. So Newell decided to set a trap for him. He borrowed a big bear trap with teeth on the jaws, cut some poles for making a V to hang a quarter of the dead cow in it, and set the trap under the meat. Then he chained the trap close to the ground around a clump of willows.

A few days later he returned to check the trap with his son Fred. Lo and behold, he had caught the bear, evidently soon after he set the trap, as the poor thing was barely breathing and near death. But it looked like a cyclone had hit the area. The ground was all torn up and the willows were chewed off until they were no more than a foot high, but the chain was so tight and close to the ground that it had not come off the willows, holding the bear fast.

Bill and his son were only a few miles from the Clint Morrison ranch, so they rode over to borrow a gun to shoot the bear with. Clint was home so he returned with the Newells only to find that the bear had died in the meantime. They figured they might as well save the hide, so young Fred was given the task of holding the horses while Bill and Clint skinned the bear. Young Fred pretty well had his hands full, as the horses were scared to death of bears and even the smell of a dead one made them spooky.

After they finished the skinning, they rolled the hide up and tied it behind Bill's saddle. The horses didn't like this one bit, but the group managed to get mounted and on their way. Clint rode with the Newells for a while and then cut off for his ranch.

Soon afterward, the middle of the green hide started to slip to one side and fell to the ground, but one paw caught in the saddle strings and hung on. That hide stretched out for ten or twelve feet, the horse stamped and it looked like it was kicking the hide about twice every jump. Well, Bill didn't stand a chance to control that horse as the two went down the side of the mountain jumping over rocks and fallen trees; all this time Fred was doing his best to keep them in sight. When they got to the foot of the mountain they were heading for a little creek bordered by willows. Just on the other side of the creek was the corner of three barbed wire fences. Well, Bill wasn't about to tackle those fences, so when he came to the creek, he reached down and got a good hold on one rein with both hands, then just as they got to the willows, he jerked the horse's nose right up in his lap which threw the horse broadside. In the process he grabbed some willows and kicked loose of the stirrups. The hide was still holding fast, so when the horse got up, he crossed the creek and headed right through two of those fences and disappeared in the dust.

Young Fred was slowed at the gate, but then rode as fast as he could in pursuit of the runaway—down the trail road to a pole gate where he finally found the horse lying on the other side after catching his knees in an attempt to jump the poles. Before Fred could catch him though, the horse was up and on his way across another wire fence, just when the saddle string broke, dumping the hide and allowing the crazed horse to go freely on his way.

Bill Newell got through the whole ordeal with little more than a few scratches from the willow brush. But the horse was never the same again. When anyone would try to ride him, they were in for a runaway, so Bill finally sold him, figuring he would never amount to "nothing".

Funny thing though, years later, when the Newell family moved east to Nebraska, their next door neighbor drove up in a buggy to welcome them to their new home. Pulling the buggy in harness was the same loco horse, looking older, but still carrying the telltale scars from the runaway ordeal, though by now he was plumb gentle.

Boom or Bust

Theodora Quimby knew it was time to pack for the 150 mile trip to San Francisco. Her baby was due and a pocket gold mine on Crocker Flat near Yosemite Valley was no place to give birth to her first child. She and her husband, Thomas, were comfortably settled on their claim on the west slope of the High Sierras, but this was the dead of winter, so she wanted to stay with relatives while she visited the doctor.

The rough stagecoach ride down the winding road caused her to go into labor, and the baby wouldn't wait. Luckily, a vacationing doctor was close by and a daughter they named Bessie was born February 23, 1987 at Big Oak Flat.

For the next two years Bessie was cared for at the mining claim while her father, Thomas Quimby, raked in the gold. He figured his discovery was bound to peter out after ten good years, so when a promoter showed him samples from the Montana gold strike, Thomas decided that this was just the chance to add to his wealth.

In the spring of 1899 he invested all his money in a partnership, packed up his family, and headed to Montana. Shortly after the family's arrival in Butte they found that the mine had been salted, and the fast-talking con man had hurriedly left town. The family was nearly broke and there was no work to be had, so with the announcement of gold strikes in eastern Oregon, Thomas decided to move the family while he still had a little money in his pocket.

The boom town of Granite seemed like their best prospect. The stage ran daily from Sumpter to Granite and the town was a flurry of freight activity. There was a merchantile, a drug store, and the Grande Hotel with its fancy dining room, saloon and game room. The family moved into the hotel and Thomas hired out as a carpenter until the placer mines opened in spring. Their life was full of promise, then tragedy struck — Thomas caught pneumonia and suddenly died.

Theodora was left with a three year-old child, little money, and no work. Her only chance to survive in this strange town was to chambermaid at the hotel and annex. it was exhausting work; cleaning dozens of rooms each day left her little time to care for Bessie. Luckily, people at the hotel were able to look after her daughter while Theodora went about her duties.

Little Bessie had no one to play with so she often followed her mother around. One day Theodora was just too busy to keep track of her, so she sent Bessie back to the hotel with strict orders, "You go straight to the hotel, and don't you get off the board walk."

Bessie left the annex, but as she came off the steps of the merchantile store there was a six-hitch freight wagon directly in her path. Now Bessie knew better than to disobey her mother so, as dozens watched in horror, she crawled between the wheels of the wagon and through the maze of horses hoofs. By some miracle none of the team spooked and Bessie crawled safely up the hotel steps as people came running from all directions.

Theodora decided that Granite was no place to raise her daughter, and a cooking job was open at Alamo, just eight miles away. This was another boom town which originated when developers sold land to gold hungry New Yorkers. There wasn't much gold, but there were swarms of miners grubbing the land.

It seemed that Alamo was a step backward—there were no board walks, and the streets were nothing but six inches of dust in dry weather and as much mud when it was wet. Worse yet, the town was full of single miners bent on raising Cain. Every payday Theodora and Little Bessie would huddle in the darkness of their tent-covered cabin—six-shooter close at hand.

The cooking job didn't last long, so Theodora decided to take in laundry. Soon she was washing for dozens of miners. Water had to be carried in buckets from Clear Creek to her cabin, then heated in a copper broiler on the wood stove. All of the dirt had to be scrubbed out by hand, rinsed out in another tub, and then finished in a bluing bath.

All of this hard work was beginning to take its toll and life kept looking more dismal for Theodora and little Bessie. That is, until one day when a local miner, Charlie Demmick, whom she met while she worked in Granite, showed up with a gold wedding band and asked for her hand in marriage. Theodora happily accepted, as this was the best gold prospect that she had seen in years.

128

Not a Laughing Matter

Back around the early 1900's, the J. H. Chambers logging camp at Star on the west slope of the Cascades, was a pretty rough place. There were usually about 100 Swedes and Irishmen working there, and they had to be tough to survive—on the job as well as off. All of the felling and bucking of trees was done by hand with a *misery whip*, and the skidding was done with oxen and a steam donkey. And, it didn't take much to start an argument, which often ended up in a real knock-down, drag-out affair.

Well, Mother McGee was the cook at the Star camp, but she could hold her own with this motley bunch, for she was as Irish as they come; she was a big woman—about 6 feet tall and around 250 pounds, but not fat. And she had a vocabulary that would just curl your hair. This she had accumulated over the years: she could just about outcuss anyone around.

One day the crew was felling trees and skidding logs right up the mountain from the cook shack. As luck would have it, one of the logs got away and was coming the full length of the mountain—heading right for the cook shack and the outbuildings. Everyone in the log's path started jumping out of the way or dove for cover. It was sheer pandemonium with all the running and hollering, because everyone on the mountain knew where it was headed. Everyone but Mother McGee, that is. She just happened to be in the outhouse at that particular moment, and hadn't heard all the commotion. The log raced down the hill and hit the outhouse squarely. The whole crew raced behind the runaway log, down the mountain at breakneck speed, expecting the worst.

When all the screamin' and ahollerin' were over, the door flew open, and there was Mother McGee with her head stuck through the hole cussin' a blue streak.

The men involved in the skidding were paralyzed with fear. None of them dared go in for supper that night, for Mother McGee would have skinned them alive!

A Bossing Dilemma

George Winfield Hastings was a natural. His English, Scotch-Irish, and Indian bloodline seemed to have given him the makings of a born leader. As long as anyone can remember, he was bossing men. If he wasn't running logging crews at Star, Rujada, or Culp Creek, he was overseeing construction of trestles and logging railroads in the Siskiyou Mountains of southern Oregon.

As a boss he had to take a strong stance, for there was always a dispute of some kind —someone either wanted his job, or they didn't like the way he was running things.

To make matters worse, crews were usually made up of differing nationalities. It seemed that the Irish were always fussing over something, so it didn't take much to start a fight. The Greeks were different in that they didn't speak English and they always wore white, which set them apart and caused a lot of bitterness in camp. As a boss, George Hastings was among the toughest; he was also one of the fairest in dealing with his men. He liked the Greeks, for they were hard workers; besides, they provided his wife a job of washing their clothes and keeping them sparkling white. This probably didn't help matters any with some of the other crews.

One time there was a big dispute. No one can remember just what it was about, but it was nearly the undoing of George and his wife. One night they both awakened out of a sound sleep, sensing that something was wrong. They discovered that someone had raised the tent siding and poured chloroform on their pillows in an attempt to kill them. Luckily they recovered, but a doctor later said that the only reason they hadn't died was that the culprit had used too much, which woke them up. No one ever figured out what the reason was for the attempt.

Another close call came after a hot, dry spell when a late evening thunderstorm built up. Lightning struck and fires popped up all over the mountain. With the wind fanning the flames, it didn't take long for the fires to spread.

George gathered the crews and rushed out to check the spread of flame. In spite of how hard the crews fought, they kept losing ground. Before long they were forced to retreat with their backs right up to the tent settlement. The fire was completely out of control and their situation seemed hopeless. George Hastings had run out of options to control this inferno. It looked certain that the flames would consume the entire camp as well as all of the men and their families, but then there was a sudden wind change and the fire took an about face, saving everyone from a fiery death.

Old White Man

From west to east, the South Grand River flows through the Dakotas on its way to join the Missouri. A short way to the south lay the rugged Buttes Badlands.

In the early 1900's a ranchhand calling himself *The Old Range Man*, pushed cattle for the Bar H Ranch. Over the years he rode many a mile of this terrain, probably topping every hill and exploring every draw until he knew the area like the back of his hand.

He told of occasional sightings of a large white wolf of whom he became rather fond, for he always referred to him as the *Old White Man*. One time the wolf stood still at the rider's approach and appeared to make tentative overtures toward friendship, with an almost imperceptible wag of his tail giving the impression that, if coaxed, he might come to him. The range rider never responded to these overtures, for who, after all, would want to make friends with a wolf?

On the moonlit night of March 12, 1912, Old White Man took a stance atop the arch of high bluffs overlooking a sheep camp. With nose pointed toward the moon, he sent his eerie cry winging skyward. Far below him the sheep were bedded for the night.

132

Alerted by the well-known howl, the herder peered out of the window of his sheep-wagon and, sure enough, there stood Old White Man vividly silhouetted in the moonlight — a tempting target. The herder couldn't let this opportunity escape him, so with one shot from his 30/30, he sent Old White Man's lifeless body hurtling down from the bluffs — forever silencing that mournful howl.

Next morn, mindful of the $5 bounty on wolves, the herder set out to find his kill and remove the ears needed to collect his bounty. To his surprise he found the carcass bearing a bronze tag inscribed: Dawson Alaska - Sled #4 - 1898 — also the address: W. O. Worland · 428 Adams Drive · Deadwood, S.D.. The creature bore all the evidence of old age — including front teeth worn to the gums, so it is quite probable that had he not been felled by the sheepherder's bullet, he would soon have died from starvation.

It seemed that the Old Range Man missed him in his wanderings over the hills, for he wrote, "His wailing moans to the sky were heard no more."

It will forever remain a mystery. Why was an Alaskan sled dog roaming the Slim Buttes Badlands of the Dakotas territory?

Montana Cayuse

Back in the days when Montana was quite young, the large cow outfits were disappearing and the homesteaders were taking over as small ranchers and farmers. Some of these newcomers were real greenhorns when it came to the ways of the West. Up on the Marias River near the old cowtown of Dupuyer, a couple of bachelors right out of the East took up a homestead and decided they were going to farm. One of the first things they needed was horses. The ones they had handled in the East were hand-raised and gentle—nothing like the wild cayuses or mustangs that were in Montana.

Well, they traded for a couple of outlaw horses that had never had a rope on them, let alone harness or saddle. They were as wild as deer, and could run like them, but when caught, they would fight like a mountain lion, kicking, biting, and striking—and they could jump a seven-foot fence without half trying.

The man that sold them the horses just ran them over to their place and put them in the corral. While the brothers were still looking over their new stock, an old cowpoke by the name of Buck rode up and said, "Well, boys, I see you got hold of some fan tails." Little did the brothers know that a fan tail is a horse that has run wild all of its life and never had its tail trimmed.

So old Buck said, "I'll git my twine down and we'll see if we can snare 'em," and added, "I don't think them critters ever been dog-corraled in their whole life."

So Buck caught them one at a time by the front feet and threw them down, got halters on, and tied them to the fence. After the Cayuses had got up and had their pull out, Buck showed the boys how to take a long pole and squeeze a wild horse up against the fence so they could get the harness on, which to a greenhorn, was quite a show.

It was standard practice with old horsemen to work a bronc with a gentle horse till they were broke, but these boys said, "Why can't we break them both at the same time?"

"Hell yes," Buck said, "Why didn't I think of it first? That is just the thing to do. Why waste your time on one when you can do 'er all at once," and at the same time you can imagine what was going on in old Buck's mind. While either one of the horses would be a man-sized job for an experienced wrangler, two of these cayuses hooked up together on a wagon would be about as uncontrollable as a cyclone.

"Well," Buck said, "I'll help ya hitch 'em up." So he showed the boys how to blindfold the cayuses so they could be led to the hitching rack without getting away.

Then Buck and the boys pushed the wagon tongue up between the cayuses and got them hooked to the wagon. That is when Buck turned to young Paul Bruner who was standing nearby, "Kid, if you never saw Barnum and Bailey's Circus, you just stick around. You are going to see something you'll remember all your life. Just keep still and out of the way."

"Well, boys," Buck said, "You get in the wagon and get comfortable and I'll untie 'em." The two boys climbed up and sat down on the spring seat; one of them took up the lines as if he were going for a joy ride. Buck went around in front, untied the horses, and took down the hitching pole and said, "Well, boys, if you are all set, I'll take off the blindfolds," and he looked at young Paul and said in a low voice, "Kid, you better get under somethin' 'cause this thing is agoin' off like a stick of dynamite, an' you might get a wagon spoke in the eye."

The second those cayuses got a spot of light, they took off like a shot. The wagon seat went over backwards, dumping the brothers to the bottom of the bed.

The rattle of the wagon was scaring the living daylights out of those cayuses and you could hear the boys hollering "Whoa!" for miles. Of course that didn't help matters any; it just scared them all the more. Those cayuses didn't have the slightest idea of what "Whoa!" meant.

They went down through the buffalo wallows on a dead run. That old wagon was up in the air more than it was on the ground—no telling what was holding it together. The boys were having a tough time just staying in the wagon, let alone ever trying to drive or stop the critters.

Old Buck was ajumpin' up and down abeatin' his hat on the ground and awhoopin' and ahollerin', "Ride 'em cowboy" at the top of his lungs, and he said, "Boy, are we amakin' history."

After the cayuses had run about three miles around the side hills, they ran into a soaphole and got stuck; they soon played out and quit fighting and floundering around. But the boys just laid flat in the bottom of the wagon, not moving or making a sound.

Back at the corral young Paul said, "Buck, what do you suppose they're adoin' now?" "Well, I don't rightly know," he said, "but I bet they're aprayin' 'Whoa'."

In a few minutes the boys got slowly out of the wagon and with caution worked their way up to the horses. They unbuckled the harness and let the horses climb out of the mud. Then they hung the harness on the wagon and started across the prairie for home.

About six weeks later, young Paul happened to see Buck in town and asked him how the "bronc busters" were getting along. "Well," he said, "The harness is still ahangin' on the wagon in the soaphole and the cayuses are still agrowin' tails. But the boys went out and bought some old nags already broke to work, to do their farmin' with."

Old Reddy and the Lamb

Ralph Bruner and his family raised cattle on Scoffin Creek along the east side of the Montana Rockies. One summer it was awfully dry so the cattle were moved to a homestead in the foothills to graze. His two sons, Harl, at age 14, and Paul, at age 11, were assigned the job to move up to an old deserted cabin to look after the stock. In those days cars were pretty rare, so the boys made the trip by team and wagon. As the cabin was quite a distance from the home ranch, the boys got to see their folks only about once a month.

Their existence was pretty grim as the furnishings were a homemade table, a bunk bed with pine boughs for mattresses, and a woodburning stove without an oven. Wooden boxes were nailed behind the stove for cupboards to hold the dishes, such as they were. Tin pots, kettles, and an old black frying pan were used for cooking. They ate from tin plates.

The boys improvised and made bread for every meal right in the top of the flour sack, by hollowing out the flour and pouring in milk, salt, lard, and baking powder. Then they slowly stirred the flour until it was the right thickness, formed it into shape, and baked it in the frying pan on the hearth of the stove with the door open.

They had the luxury of a milk cow they called Old Reddy. She would come up to the back door of the cabin every night and morning for her grain and to be milked.

During the summer a band of sheep passed by and left a lamb stranded nearby. The boys took it to the cabin and raised it on a bottle, and gave her the name of Punkins.

One night Harl was getting supper, so it was Paul's turn to milk the cow and feed the lamb. He had just started milking Old Reddy when Punkins came around for her supper. Now, Paul didn't like milk to start with, so he said to himself, "Here's a chance to get rid of some of these chores." So, he coaxed Punkins around behind Old Reddy and introduced her to the natural way of life. She took right ahold and everything went fine, that is, until the source of supply began to give out and she tried to solve the problem by giving a big butt. Old Reddy looked back and saw her and that's when things began to happen. The back door to the cabin was open, so Old Reddy took off on a beeline for the opening, with Punkins right on her heels, and in they went.

When Harl, who was in the cabin cooking, saw them coming, he let out a big yell, which just speeded Old Reddy up as if the Devil was on her tail. She couldn't get around the table, so she went over the top, upsetting the whole thing in a heap. Harl let fly with the frying pan to head her off, but when she turned for the door, there stood Punkins, big as life. Well, not wanting anything more to do with the darned sheep, Old Reddy changed her mind about going out the door.

So Paul ran around the cabin to open the front door. With the table upset in the middle of the room, the shortest route was around the stove. That would have been fine if there was enough room to fit a cow between the stove and the cupboards, but there wasn't. So down came the whole shebang with a deafening crash—the cupboards with all the pots and pans on one side and the stovepipe full of soot on the other.

Well, by that time the air was so full of smoke, soot, and noise, that the brothers couldn't see or hear a thing. By then Old Reddy was lined up with the front door and on her way in high gear. The front door was only half as wide as the back door, so about half-way through she got stuck. There's no telling what goes on in a cow's mind under such circumstances, but, by the way she was kicking, bucking, and bawling, one would have thought that the lamb was a mountain lion ready to spring on her back. Probably, her only thought was to get through that opening as fast as possible and head for the brush before anything else happened.

Before the door jamb gave way and let her go, she managed to give the whole cabin a green grass Kalsomine job to top off the rest of the damage. The last sight of Old Reddy was that she was still running towards the far corner of the field, a mile away.

After the excitement died down, the brothers returned to the cabin to survey the damage. There was their supper, a sack of flour, and their dishes all in a heap and covered with soot, and the leavings of Old Reddy. It sure was a mess.

Harl turned to his brother and said, "If you think for one minute that cleaning up this mess will be easier than feeding Punkins, by golly, I'll feed that sheep myself from now on."

As for Old Reddy, she was never quite the same. It was days before she returned to the cabin for her grain. And she kept very alert to anything suspicious forevermore.

The Meanest Cow Alive

Margrita Hastings was good with horses, but she never could milk worth a hoot, so her mother usually took on the chore with old Flossie. Now that cow was always a problem; if she wasn't trying to kick the bucket over, she was swishing her crappy tail in someone's face. Margrita's mother had had just about enough of this so her husband asked her why she didn't tie the tail to the cow's leg. Now everyone knew that old Flossie would never go for that, so he thought he would solve the problem by getting a piece of brick and tying that to the cow's tail to keep it from swinging. He knew better than that, but not to the extent that he realized the strength that old Flossie had—one swing with that brick-laden tail catching him along side the head and he dropped right to the floor—out colder than a mackerel.

Old Flossie would usually pick her times to act her worst. One Saturday night the family was planning to go to town—mother and the kids to the movie house and father to meet his cronies in the local saloon. For Margrita, this was something special, because William S. Hart was playing, and she just loved to see western movies.

Well, it was time for milking and old Flossie picked this occasion to act up—she just was not going to go into the barn. The more everyone tried, the wilder she got. After several attempts of chasing that old cow up and down the road by the river, Margrita was so mad that she could spit nails, for she just knew that they would be too late for the movie. She figured time was a-wasting, so, picking up a rock—against her mother's warning—she let fly, catching old Flossie right in the head. Well, that old cow went down and her eyes rolled back in her head. Margrita's mother was screaming, "I warned you that you were going to kill her."

But, luckily, old Flossie managed to get up and go into the barn without further trouble. She was even pretty cooperative with the milking that night, so Margrita didn't miss the picture show after all.

Luck Run Out

One night Lady Luck stepped out on 16 year-old Charley Hastings.

He and a couple of his friends rode into town under threatening skies. They left their horses at the livery stable and proceeded to take in the sights of the visiting Chautauqua tent show.

It had rained during the evening and the ground was slick as grease. Just as they were leaving the livery, Charley's horse slipped and fell in the middle of the street. It all happened so suddenly that he couldn't get his foot out of the stirrup, causing him to get caught under the full weight of his horse, busting his knee.

It was a terrible break and for weeks Charley hobbled around on crutches. The doctors didn't like the way the knee was healing, so they decided to rebreak the leg and set it again. Time didn't seem to help and the doctors repeated the procedure once more, with the same unsuccessful result. When they announced that they would have to do it a third time, Charley grabbed them by their collars and told them flat out that he wasn't going to stand for any more of their treatment.

As he was going down the street on his crutches, an old man approached him and said, "Son, a big stong fellow like you shouldn't have to hobble around on those sticks for so long. You get yourself some Absorbine Horse Liniment and use it faithfully, every day for a long time."

Charley figured he didn't have anything to lose, so he tried the remedy. In a few weeks his leg started improving. After a while it got so much better that he was able to get rid of the crutches. By the time he was ready to graduate from school, his leg was nearly as good as new.

Charley's first job after graduation was working in the woods, felling trees and bucking logs. His leg never gave him much problem, so he started logging full time.

About 18 years later, while bucking timber on a steep hillside, he was having trouble getting a log bucked through, so he climbed down on the lower side. Now, he knew this was a bad deal—to get on the downhill side of a log—but there was a big root holding it in place and he figured he was plenty safe.

As he was nearly finished sawing, the log suddenly gave way and started to roll. He tried to jump into a hole in the ground, but the weak knee gave out, causing him to fall into the path of the runaway log. Life and luck ran out on Charley Hastings that day.

Around the Town
&
The Leisure Life

Boom towns sprung up with each new gold strike.

Mining camp at Cornucopia, Oregon — 1884.

Company towns centered around the sawmills.

Cattletowns provided supplies and entertainment for the cowboy.

Malheur City, Oregon.

Fire caused an instant facelift of many towns throughout the West.

Fire on Sumpter, Oregon mainstreet — 1917.

Sturdier buildings and a coat of paint came with the rebuilding.

Hillsboro, North Dakota mainstreet.

Brick replaced the wood as growth ensued and towns prospered.

A one-roomed schoolhouse went with an established community.

High Valley, Oregon school—ca. 1895.

Everyone decked out in their finest for the Sabbath.

Any town of some size formed their own ball team for the competition.

Croquet clubs were the social event of the day.

Bicycling was a favorite afternoon pastime.

Camping was a welcome getaway from the daily grind.

Skiing was reserved for the more adventurous souls.

Winter travel was little problem with a horse and cutter.

Card playing is age-old as an engaging pasttime.

Stopping at the local watering hole never went out of style.

Saloon at Denio—on the Nevada-Oregon border.

The President's Cigar

After momentous service in the Civil War, James Allison was offered the opportunity of an appointment to Annapolis and West Point on succeeding days. He finally decided on West Point, probably because he had served under his father who was a Colonel of the Seventeenth Kentucky Regiment.

Like other plebes at the military school, he was unmercifully hazed by the upper classmen. That is until they learned of his war experience; then they had more respect for him, even though he was still young enough not to have shaven yet.

One of his classmates was Fred Grant, son of the President of the United States. Fred frequently got permission to visit his father and would return from his White House visit with a handful of gorgeous gold-wrapped White House cigars which he would pass out among his friends.

Allison was given one of these cigars just before his furlough, and was treasuring it to smoke on the way home.

After boarding the train he headed straight to the smoking car. As he entered, he could see it was crowded, with only one vacant seat next to a little old lady. Allison sat next to her and hoped that another seat would soon be vacated as he didn't wish to disturb her. But, they passed station after station and no one got off.

Finally, he could stand it no longer. He turned to her and said, "Madam, do you object to a cigar?"

"Well," she said, "I usually smoke a pipe when I'm home, but if ye've got a cigar, I'd be glad to have it."

He politely forked it over and sat back in chagrin as he watched the little old lady savor President Grant's cigar for the rest of the trip.

Eat My Dust

Ellen Jones took great pride in having some of the best horse flesh that Missourians had ever seen. She and her horses were well known for miles around. Next to her family, raising and training horses was her first love.

One bright sunny day she thought it would be grand to visit her neighbor whose house was a few miles down the road, so she got all decked out and hitched up two of her finest for the trip.

She and her daughter, Mamie, were having a spritely ride when a gent and his team approached from behind and started trotting alongside to pass.

Quick as a flash Ellen Jones was standing up in the buggy cracking her whip, and the horses were off and running. She wasn't about to give way to this gent and his team—nobody, but nobody passed Ellen Jones and her finest. It was all matter of principle to her.

She laid the whip over the horses ears and cried out to get them moving. The team took off like a shot, so fast that it was like the devil was after them. On they ran, with young Mamie pleading for her life. Her mother called out, "Turn around Mamie and see if he is gaining on us!"

Poor Mamie was hanging on for dear life. By the time she could finally glance over one shoulder, all she could see was a speck in the distance.

The gent had stopped a quarter mile back, tied his horses up, gotten out of the rig, and was heading toward the house.

Mother Jones was in Seventh Heaven, but poor Mamie had one more reason to hate horses for the rest of her life.

Billy the Bear Cub

There wasn't much entertainment for young boys living in the Blue Moutains of Oregon so, when Bill Wetzel had a chance to buy a bear cub from his neighbor, he didn't hesitate a second. He knew this would be the best thing he could do to keep his two sons, Lew and Eddy, occupied and out of trouble. The boys were thrilled at having a bear they could call their own, and promptly named him *Billy*.

Without delay they started working with him, and within days had the little cub leading like a dog, at the end of a leash. Then with some coaxing and lots of treats, they got him to sitting up on command and begging for food.

They never teased him, so Billy never got mean, becoming more like a dog than the bear that he was. When he was not with the two boys he was kept chained to the base of a large pine tree behind the house.

One day Billy got tired of just lying around, so he climbed up on one side of a dead limb and came down on the other side. But when he reached the end of the chain he lost his grip on the tree and ended up hanging from his neck, with his rump a couple of feet off the ground. When the boys heard his cries and saw his predicament, they ran out to save him. Lew grabbed a pole and knocked the dead limb off, dropping the cub to the ground, bottom first.

Poor Billy must have been hurt from the impact, for he whimpered a bit and then lay down. The boys petted him and pampered him with food and water which seemed to finally cause him to forget his injury.

After he healed up the boys figured he needed some exercise, so Lew rigged a harness for the cub. Then the two put a pair of shafts on their play-wagon so they could hitch Billy to it and drive him around. The boys got the bear hitched up without much trouble, and Eddy got in the wagon to take the first ride. But as soon as he started, Billy became scared of the wagon that was rattling and following behind him. He took off as fast as he could, right out across the railroad tracks. The wagon started to come apart as it struck the first set of rails, dumping Eddy out in a sprawling heap in the dust. The cub disappeared into a pine thicket and was nowhere to be found. Parts of the wagon and harness had hung up and torn loose as the cub raced wildly among the trees and brush. The boys searched the forest for hours but failed to locate any sign of their bear.

Finally they headed home, feeling downhearted, for they figured they would never see Billy again. When they reached the house, they broke the sad news to their mother. After listening patiently, she said, "Look out in the back yard." There was Billy, chained to the tree where she had fastened him, sleeping peacefully after he returned home from the wild ordeal.

One-Room Schoolhouse

November 20, 1920 was a red-letter day for Dorothy Bruner, for she had her first job—a contract to teach in a one-room schoolhouse with a salary of one hundred and twenty dollars a month. Even though the pay wasn't much, the teacher in this community was held in rather high esteem.

Dorothy didn't think she had much of a chance for the job, for she remembered her grandfather saying, "It's a waste of money for her to continue schooling; she'll probably marry a farmer anyway." But, she now finished high school and there was such a shortage of teachers that many special permits were issued to fill rural schools, and she was one of the lucky ones.

The little Moulton school east of Ledger, Montana was supported by local farmers who were often under terrible burdens to make ends meet, let alone build and support a school. Like most of the other rural schools, it served as a community center. People would come from miles around for a weekend dance in the schoolhouse. A prosperous school might have a piano, but usually music was supplied by a local fiddler and organist. Babies were put to bed on the teacher's desk in the corner, and mothers had to keep a watchful eye that none were smothered under the pile of coats. Everyone contributed a cake or sandwiches for a snack; coffee was made in a wash boiler and served in tin cups. Nothing was very fancy, but everyone seemed to have a grand time. On Sundays the school reverted to church services and Sunday school, and during elections it became the area's polling place.

Now, as a teacher with thirteen pupils in five grades, Dorothy remembered back when she was a student. She wondered if the favorite winter sport was still placing snowballs on the rafters above the teacher's chair? She recognized most of the books on the small library shelf, since only a few new ones had been added over the years. Teaching shouldn't be too hard since most of the text books and methods hadn't changed since she had first attended school. Her greatest concern was how she would be graded since teachers of that era were judged by the parents—usually on two scores—how good the Christmas program was and if the seventh and eighth graders passed the state exams.

The winter of 1920-21 was a cold one. Many a morning Dorothy had to walk the mile to school over frozen fields in below zero weather. She had to start out early enough in order to build a fire so there was a little circle of warmth for the children when they arrived. The sides of the stove would be red hot in its effort to push back the awful cold and it was usually noon before the children could move comfortably to their seats.

The spring of '21 wasn't any better. A black blizzard hit the school one day about noon. The Russian thistles were blowing horizontally past the windows. By one o'clock they couldn't see across the road, and at three it was too dark to read. The older boys were disgusted when they were not allowed to start out alone, but Dorothy insisted that they stay with the group and hold on to the little ones. Everyone had to face the awful blowing soil as they struggled down the road. One neighbor tried to reach the group in his Case roadster but he couldn't hear them or see them in the storm. Finally, after the wind subsided, he returned to find Miss Bruner with all her pupils waiting in the middle of the road. There they stood—covered with dirt, hair matted, and their faces mud-streaked from their tearing eyes. They survived the storm, but they were a sorry sight.

A Short-Lived Entrepreneurship

Edward Wetzel could hardly wait for the 4th of July to come around. For weeks he had been experimenting with various mixtures of black powder and charcoal poured into sections of bamboo fishing poles, attempting to create the perfect skyrocket.

He learned a few secrets from the Japanese section hands who worked the tracks in the Oregon's Blue Mountains. They were proficient at making Roman candles from the powder of railroad fuses, but they didn't have much experience with skyrockets.

Young Edward found that if he used too much charcoal, the rockets barely lifted out of the vertical trough-launcher guide, arced over, and fell back to earth. Too much powder and the rockets exploded.

Come the 4th he was ready for the celebration. As night approached he placed his rocket in the launching trough, lit the rice paper fuse, and beat a hasty retreat to get away in case he loaded too much of the powder.

The rocket blasted off and lifted smoothly, leaving a trail of flame and sparks as it streaked into the nighttime sky. He was elated—it was a spectacular success.

The next day he gathered up all of the burntout cases that he could find; he was in the business of making skyrockets. His youngest brother got curious with what was going on, so while Edward was busy working, little Guy poured some gunpowder out of a can into a pile on the boardwalk and proceeded to light it without getting back. Little did he know the power of the blackpowder as he squatted over it. The powder disappeared in a flash of light and smoke, burning the little boy badly about the face and hands. Luckily he must have closed his eyes as he touched the match to the powder, for he didn't loose his eyesight, but he singed his eyebrows and the skin peeled off his face and hands, fortunately healing without any sign of lasting scars.

Needless to say, their father was upset. He dumped all of Edward's precious mixes and gunpowder in the creek, and burned all of the rocket cases and launcher troughs. He didn't whip Edward, but he brought his experimenting to a screeching halt and promptly put him out of the rocket business.

Strange Happenings

In the late 1890's the Jones family lived up on Quartz Creek, a God-forsaken place in the Siskiyou Mountains of southern Oregon.

Now Mother Jones was always having some kind of spiritual experience which caused untold friction in the family because her husband didn't believe in any kind of spiritualism,whatsoever, nor did their daughter, Mamie.

But Mother Jones lived for the times when she could invite all of her believer friends over for a private seance though she had to wait until her husband was going to be gone, and she couldn't have Mamie involved in the sessions because she always broke the spell.

In fact Mother Jones got so involved with the spirits that she finally had to give it up—the spirits got to bothering her too much, especially when they began tapping at the head of the bed in the middle of the night.

Well, family life was going along pretty smoothly, that is, until one summer evening when Father Jones was returning home along a narrow woodland path when he felt something reach out and touch him on the shoulder.

"Frank?" he called out, thinking his eldest son was playing tricks on him. There was no answer.

"Fred?" he asked, thinking that it might be his other son.

He jawed at them a little bit, thinking that they were still trying to play some tricks. But still there was no answer.

He continued on his way, when suddenly he was touched on the shoulder again, and a voice drifted out of the darkness, "Come this way."

Now, being a Welshman, he wasn't easily frightened, but he was going to have it out with his sons as soon as he got home. As he opened the door, there were his two boys sitting in front of the fire. Upon inquiring how long they had been there, his wife said that they hadn't left the house since the afternoon.

All that evening he sat quietly, a finger up alongside his nose, staring into the fire.

About bedtime, he said to his wife, "Tonight I got a summons; I'm going to die. You have been after me for years to join the church, so I think I will." She was shocked speechless, as this was so out of character for him.

Not long afterward he did join the church, and faithfully attended services.

Then one afternoon he was sitting alone in the breezeway while his wife was busy in the kitchen. Suddenly, the image of a young child appeared coming from the kitchen door, across the breezeway, and stopped right in front of him. It was Clytie, his favorite son who died before reaching his second birthday. Father Jones reached out to placed his hand on Clytie's head, and then the image disappeared.

He interpreted this as another omen that he had better get right, and when he told Mother Jones about the apparition she didn't doubt it one bit.

Shortly afterward he suddenly left for California without any explanation and his family never saw him again. A while later they learned that his premonition had come to pass when news was received that he had died from the Black Pneumonia.

Barnstorming Days

The bi-wing Jennie circling overhead caught the young boy's attention and enthralled him; never had he seen anything like it before. He frantically ran in circles as the plane went around and around; the loud bark of the engine as the plane dipped low overhead dropping leaflets excited him into a frenzy. Rumor had it that a few were lucky ones entitling the bearer to a free ride. Boys all around the town diligently searched the streets, alleys, and yards, fighting over any paper found. No sooner had the leaflets settled than a group of World War I fighter types began displaying mock combat maneuvers and individual aerial stunts over the town.

This was just too much for Eugene Clay; he had to see those aircraft up close. After persistent nagging, his father loaded the family into the Model-T Ford and they set out to find the right pasture among the forest clumps which beautified the Grande Ronde Valley in the early 1920's. Around sundown, a landing plane showed them the way. They came to a fence where many other cars were parked with people admiring a line of varied types of aircraft belonging to one of the flying circuses which toured the country after the First World War.

Young Clay was in Seventh Heaven—there were Curtiss JN-4Ds, a Spad, a Hanriot, and a Fokker D-VII with checkered paint design. His dream ended with his father's sharp summons to crank up the Ford so that they could get home before dark.

It seems that people all over the valley got caught up in the thrill of the daily aerial activity. Some of Eugene's friends from the Imbler area were among men and boys riding on a flat-bed truck taking them out to see the planes one day, when they crossed a railroad track in front of a speeding train. Everyone was looking up at a plane flying overhead and did not see the train, and most of them were killed.

This was a sobering event for the boy and the town, but it wasn't long before he got caught up in the excitement again when a neighbor lady called out over the fence. "Oh! Eugene, I bet you don't know what I saw down where the tracks cross Fir Street."

Without hesitation, he ran down the street to find an open freight car with the fuselage of an airplane standing beside it on its landing gear and tail skid. A group of men were still unloading wing and tail panels. With eager curiosity, he and some other boys climbed up into the freight car and began examining the contents. Everyone lent a willing hand, unpacking plane parts and carrying everything down the street to the local Hudson car garage.

As it turned out, two war surplus Standard J-1s had been purchased and were to be assembled right there in town to start the area's first aviation company.

While the assembling progressed, the town should have declared a holiday, as most businesses were deserted while their operators, along with idle men and boys, pressed in on workers so heavily that the big mechanic in charge had to constantly threaten them to stay out of the way. Eugene spent as much time as he could hanging around the Hudson garage, learning about the finer points of aircraft assembly, but he missed the big day when the planes were taken to the field and tested. His school attendance caused him to miss all of the early flights, so he began to plead with his father again for another trip out to the field where the planes were kept.

The following evening the well-loaded Ford once again chugged out to the magic pasture. There among the wild flowers of spring sat the object of the boy's affection, but much larger and grander than he had imagined. The Standard, with its big 150 hp Hispano-Suiza engine, seem to tower over the crowd that engulfed it.

Eugene and his brother jumped out of the car and rushed over to join the throng. His eyes devoured every minute detail as he looked up at that new, shiny airplane. The nose was cocked up at a rakish angle emphasizing its beautifully cowled engine and gleaming mahogany propeller. The wings had the creamy yellow tinge of clear-dope fabric, the struts were polished mahogany, and the cockpit cowling was blue. The inside was padded with laced brown leather. Neatly stenciled on the brown fuselage side of the plane was the name "La Grande Aircraft Company."

Then came the action. The big mechanic ordered everyone back. As two men lifted the tail around, wedge-shaped blocks were placed in front of the wheels, the dashing pilot climbed into the cockpit, and the mechanic swung the propeller. The yelling back and forth of "Switch Off!" and "Contact!" added to the excitement. With a thunderous roar, the big engine started, and in a second everyone around was covered with dust and weeds. By the time they wiped their eyes and the dust had cleared, the plane was waddling down the rough pasture. The pilot turned into the wind and then accelerated with a rush into the air. Banking in a turn to clear the trees, the plane headed toward town, growing smaller in the distance—then suddenly it was larger and getting lower in its glide toward the field. The pilot had to be good, for the landing was very soft, and Eugene could hardly tell when the plane touched ground.

With the setting of the sun, the fathers began rounding up all of the boys, but it was hard to break them away. As Eugene cranked up the Ford and climbed in over the side, he remembers his dad saying, "Well! I hope you have had your stomach full of airplanes." He seemed very disappointed at his son's strong negative reaction.

The summer came on and there was rarely a day that Eugene didn't see a plane flying overhead, but he didn't get another chance to get out to the airfield as it was located far beyond the other side of town. Some of his friends did get out there on their bicycles, but Eugene hadn't stacked enough firewood to earn the money for a bike, so he never made it to the field again.

Toward the end of summer he and his brother were playing outside in the last shred of daylight as kids do, when they heard the welcome roar of an airplane engine. Suddenly the black shape of the diving airplane appeared, followed by another. They leveled out and disappeared into the dusk, and the last that the two boys saw of them was fading pinpoints of fire from the engines' exhaust.

A couple of days later, there was a story in the local paper to the effect that the pilots and mechanic had disappeared, owing considerable money to several businessmen in town. It seemed that the La Grande Aircraft Company was no more.

The Town Scoundrel

Cottage Grove probably wasn't much different than most other towns in the 1920's, especially in its characters. It seems that every town had at least one in that day and age.

Clyde Hastings was one that just never grew up. His nieces and nephews loved his antics and could never understand why the grownups were everlastingly disgusted with him, as there were always funny times when he was around.

Uncle Clyde never took things too seriously; and perhaps, to the children, they didn't think or care about the serious things in life.

During Prohibition times he was seen around town pushing a large wicker baby buggy, often with one or two kids in tow. The local lawmen never did discover that this was his favorite method to earn money, for who would ever dream that under the snugly-wrapped baby was a buggy full of booze.

Sometimes he changed his method of distribution to his clientele, and sometimes he got outright careless, which usually ended in his arrest. This resulted in a late-night call to his brother requesting funds to bail him out. Little wonder that his relatives were a little disgusted with his actions.

But, in spite of these *slight* infractions with the law, he was quite harmless and had a heart of gold.

Several years later his true character came to light when a drunk was erratically driving down the town's main street and headed straight for the sidewalk. Without hesitation, Clyde jumped in front of the car to push his daughter out of the way — thus saving her life as well as her unborn child's — but forfeiting his in the process.

Attacked by Mashers

Al Young was extremely proud of the four horses he used for hauling machinery to the mines in the mountains around Sumpter. One of the horses, Kate, was always giving him some kind of trouble when he was breaking the team to work. She was a big bay mare who was nervous and high strung, so he purposely put her in the wheel on the off side, which is teamster's jargon for the right rear position in a team of four or more horses.

That winter of 1916 the snow was deep, the sleighing was good, and there were kids galore taking advantage of the prime conditions. Al was returning from one of his trips to the mines. His sled empty as he drove into town.

Now he could have turned on one of the lower streets and avoided Main Street altogether, but he wasn't about to, not with four beautiful young horses that he had trained to move out as proudly as though they were pulling the King's coach. He wasn't about to go sneaking up any back streets. No Siree! Right toward the center of town he drove, with the high-stepping horses making a wide turn onto the hard-packed snow of Main Street. People on both sides stared like they were watching a parade.

Too bad it had to happen: a small boy sliding down a coasting hill couldn't get stopped and slid right into the hind legs of the big bay mare. Kate jumped about as high as the second story of the hotel and came down running, miraculously missing the youngster. The other three spirited horses sprang into action, and they were hitting top speed as they passed the drug store. By the time they got to the post office, the big sled was sailing in the air, coming down only to lightly caress the snow now and then.

Just as Al Young's beautiful four came tearing close to the intersection, the widow Beach, a pious lady whose gaze was usually trained skyward, started to cross the street to avoid walking in front of the corner saloon. Two husky young miners coming out of the saloon saw her, ran after her, and pulled her back to the safety of the sidewalk. The dear little lady, still unmindful of the coming danger, screamed, kicked, and tried to scratch the faces of her rescuers.

The horses were still running out of control, and Al was sure they would try to turn right at the end of the street, but there he executed a skillful maneuver. Just as they started the turn, he yanked hard on the bridle of the off leader and snapped the whip over the rump of the near leader. That threw the two leaders and Kate into the snowbank by the right side of the road. The near wheeler was the only one left standing in the street, though he was strapped tight in the rigging. Al held all of them there until they quieted, then he let them struggle out and head home to the barn.

The widow Beach told her story many times. She never mentioned the runaway horses, but only that she had been grabbed by two young men right in broad daylight. Some of her friends thought they could even detect a note of pride in her voice.

Historical Notes

❧ Story Notes ❧

Settling In.....

A New Home—Ernest and Edna McIntire's move to Colorado in 1918 where they farmed until 1957, when they moved to Wray. Story by their daughter, June McIntire Schrib.

Calves Have Cold Noses—A humorous episode of raising chickens on the east slope of Montana's Rockies. Adapted from Paul Bruner's story in *The Bruner Bunch*, courtesy of Dorothy Bruner Floerchinger.

Everything but a Match—The story of two sisters who homesteaded in eastern Montana in the late 1800's, courtesy of Dorothy Bruner Floerchinger.

A Close Call—Bill Newell's brush with death while trying to save his cattle in a Wyoming blizzard. Adapted from a story by his daughter, Edith Newell Perkins.

Everlasting Lessons—Ralph Bruner's childhood encounter with a cougar in the forests around Idaho's Camas Prairie in the 1880's. Adapted from *"The Bruner Bunch"* from Dorothy Bruner Floerchinger.

The Threat of Wolves—Adapted from Altamae Wyncoop Van Sant's childhood experiences with wolves in the Little Powder River area of Wyoming.

Turned Away—Marietta McCubbin and her sick child were turned away from the Richardson fort during the Indian scare of 1878. Adapted from a story from Carman Pearce, wife of Mrs. McCubbin's grandson.

Skirmishes.....

It Pays to be Short—James Allison's brush with death after enlisting as a drummer boy in the Civil War. Adapted from Col. Philip Allison's reminiscences of his father, courtesy of Jordis Schick.

Devil Horse—Adapted from Brigadier General James N. Allison's experiences in the 2nd Cavalry at old Fort Laramie during the Indian Wars. Courtesy of Jordis Schick.

Savage Justice—A tragic episode on the Fassett wagon train enroute to California in 1850. Adapted from documentation sent by Marjorie Wilson of her great-great-grandmother's trip across the plains.

A Charmed Life—Walter Braten's adventures on the Indian Frontier during the latter years of 1800. Adapted from documents sent by Lila M. Crawford about her great-uncle's life on the western fontier.

Prisoner of War—The imprisonment of a wounded Indian maiden following Col. Miles' mid-winter attack on the Sioux. Adapted from General James N. Allison's experiences, courtesy of Jordis Schick.

A Plan Gone Awry—The ill-fated robbery of Union Pacific train no. 5 during the summer of 1914. Adapted from Edward Wetzel's experiences in *"Mountain Trails and Iron Rails"*, courtesy of Vera Hearing.

On the Move.....

A Reluctant Move—Mamie Jones' reluctant decision to marry her fiance and move from the comfort of civilization to the wild backwoods of Oregon. From Margrita Balcom's reminiscence of her parent's move from Cameron, Missouri where her father broke horses for the Army.

Lost in a Blizzard—Sid Wetzel's hazardous journey to reach home on Montana's Milk River ahead of a storm. Adapted from his brother's writings in *"Mountain Trails and Iron Rails"*, courtesy of Vera Hearing.

The Rawhide Railroad—Dorsey Baker's plot to make his fortune by constructing the first railroad in the Northwest. Adapted from Edward Wetzel's writings courtesy of his niece, Vera Hearing.

Cherokee Run—Winfied and Elizabeth Hastings' decision to homestead on the Cherokee Strip after years of roaming in a covered wagon. From Margrita Balcom's reminiscences of her grandparents' experiences.

Too Much Speed—The tragic train wreck in Oregon's Blue Mountains the winter of 1910. Adapted from Edward Wetzel's *"Mountain Trails and Iron Rails"* courtesy of his niece, Vera Hearing.

California, Here We Come!—The John Bruner family experiences in moving from their drought-stricken wheat farm in Washington. Adapted from *"The Bruner Bunch"* courtesy of Dorothy Bruner Floerchinger.

The Wrangler's Last Ride—The final episode in Wrangler Dave's life in the South Grand River of the Dakotas. As written by his neighbor, Maizie Carr.

Day by Day.....

A Most Memorable Fourth—Adapted from Berenice Bue Juve's frightening childhood experience while her parents were away from the ranch for the 4th of July celebration in Wallowa, Oregon.

Bear Loco—Bill Newell's bout with a rogue bear that killed one of his cows in the foothills of the Laramie Mountains of Wyoming. Adapted from Fred Newell's story, courtesy of his sister, Edith Newell Perkins.

Boom or Bust—Theodora Quimby's hardships of raising a daughter alone in the wild boom towns on the mining frontier, as told by that daughter, Bessie Quimby Greene.

Not a Laughing Matter—Mother McGee's near tragic episode with a runaway log in the J.H. Chambers logging camp in early 1900. From reminiscences of Margrita Balcom.

A Bossing Dilemma—George Hastings' close call with death while bossing crews for the railroad around the turn-of-the-century. From reminiscences of his daughter, Margrita Hastings Balcom.

Old White Man—Seaborn Ledbetter's experience with an old wolf that roamed the Slim Buttes Badlands of the Dakotas in the early 1900's. Adapted from a story by Mazie Carr.

Montana Cayuse—An escapade of an old horse wrangler helping a couple of greenhorn brothers break a pair of cayuse horses to harness. Adapted from Paul Bruner's story, courtesy of Dorothy Bruner Floerchinger.

Old Reddy and the Lamb—A wild fracas resulting from young Paul Bruner's attempt to ease his evening chores. Adapted from *"The Bruner Bunch"* courtesy of Dorothy Bruner Floerchinger.

The Meanest Cow Alive—An infuriating episode of the Hastings family with Flossie, their milk cow. As told by Margrita Hastings Balcom.

Luck Run Out—Charley Hastings' brushes with Lady Luck and the tragic day when she left him while he was logging in central Oregon. As told by his sister, Margrita Hastings Balcom.

Around the Town & The Leisure Life.....

The President's Cigar—The backfiring of James Allison's plan to savor a cigar from President Grant. Adapted from his experience upon graduation from West Point; courtesy of Jordis Schick.

Eat My Dust—Ellen Jones just didn't have it in her soul for anyone around Cameron Missouri to pass up her high-stepping team. Margrita Balcom's reminiscences of her grandmother.

Billy the Bear Cub—The Wetzel brothers' shenanigans of raising a pet bear in Oregon's Blue Mountains. Adapted from Edward Wetzel's *"Mountain Trails and Iron Rails"*, courtesy of his niece, Vera Hearing.

One-Room Schoolhouse—Dorothy Bruner Floerchinger's first teaching experience in the little Moulton, Montana schoolhouse. Adapted from her story in *"The Bruner Bunch"* family history.

A Short-Lived Entrepreneurship—Edward Wetzels's scheme for a spectacular first business brought to a screeching halt before it had much of a chance. Adapted from his writings, courtesy of Vera Hearing.

Strange Happenings—Unexplained incidents in the life of Pierce and Ellen Jones while living in Oregon's Rogue River country near Merlin in the 1890's. As told by their granddaughter, Margrita Balcom.

Barnstorming Days—Young Eugene Clay's infatuation with the traveling air circus that came to town. Adapted from his writing about early-day flying. His infatuation continues today through fine art and model renderings, with works hung in the Smithsonian Institute and the Air Force Academy.

The Town Scoundrel—Clyde Hastings' caper during prohibition times of the 1920's around Cottage Grove, Oregon; as told by his niece, Margarita Hastings Balcom.

Attacked by Mashers—Widow Beach's narrow escape from imminent danger from Al Young's runaway team the winter of 1915. Adapted from the story written by his son, Frederick Young.

◈ *Photographic Illustrations* ◈

Jerry & Cathy Gildemeister
Author & Publisher

Jerry and Cathy have a home-based studio that is shared with their cat, Miss Poo, in the sagebrush foothills of Oregon's Wallowa Mountains. Jerry is the designer and co-author of **Rendezvous, Traces, Where Rolls the Oregon, A Letter Home,** and the **Union Centennial Album.** He and Cathy worked together to create **An American Vignette,** with Cathy specializing in the photo image presentation. In addition to publishing under the sign of the *Bear Paw,* they devote much of their time to illustrative photography, publication design, and providing consultation and production services for clients wishing to self-publish. They are currently working on several projects to add to their growing list of limited edition book publications.

The Bear Wallow Story

The Bear Wallow Publishing Company was formed to help preserve our Western Heritage through finely crafted limited edition printings. The first book printed under the sign of the *Bear Paw* was **Rendezvous** just 10 years ago. Then followed **Traces, Where Rolls the Oregon,** and **A Letter Home.** Bear Wallow publications are created for those readers and collectors who appreciate the enduring beauty of finely crafted, edition-bound books. We strive for excellence in publishing. Our pledge to the reader: to maintain high artistic quality, historic accuracy, and fine printing to assure that each volume is a true work of art. Bear Wallow books are perfect for gift giving and are increasing in demand by collectors of rare and unique books.

Carrying on this distinctive tradition is **An American Vignette.**

❧ In Parting ❧

    With this 10th year of publishing, I wish to thank all of the Irwin-Hodson and Lincoln & Allen production staff for their involvement in our projects, with a special note of appreciation for the craftmanship of George Brummer & Bob Koppler for the printing preparation, and Steven Orlowski, Frank Deusser, & Mike Kleifges for the press work involved on **An American Vignette** *and* **A Letter Home**.....*and finally, a very special thank you to my wife, partner and co-worker—Cathy, who made this project possible. I am especially grateful for the long hours she endured in the darkroom to create the photo imagery from originals that have suffered damage and deterioration over time.*

    Only through this dedication and skill is it possible to present the quality reproduction for this lasting tribute to our Western Heritage.

Jerry Gildemeister

THE BEAR WALLOW PUBLISHING COMPANY
10th ANNIVERSARY
UNION OREGON
1978 – 1988